BIBLE
PROMISES

BIBLE
PROMISES

WHITAKER
HOUSE

All Scriptures are from the King James Version of the Holy Bible.

BIBLE PROMISES

ISBN: 0-88368-765-8
Printed in the United States of America
© 1995 by Whitaker House

Whitaker House
30 Hunt Valley Circle
New Kensington, PA 15068
www.whitakerhouse.com

Library of Congress Cataloging-in-Publication Data

Bible. English. Selections. 2002.
Bible promises.
p. cm.
ISBN 0-88368-765-8 (pbk.)
1. Bible—Quotations. I. Title.
BS416 .B5213 2002
220.5'2036—dc21
2002004939

2 3 4 5 6 7 8 9 10 11 12 **WH** 11 10 09 08 07 06 05 04

Contents

Bible Promises for Those Who Are... 113

Introduction

*According as his divine power hath given
unto us all things that pertain unto life and
godliness, through the knowledge of him
that hath called us to glory and virtue:
whereby are given unto us*
exceeding great and precious promises*:
that by these ye might be partakers of the divine
nature, having escaped the corruption
that is in the world through lust.*
—2 Peter 1:3-4

G od has given a rich inheritance of spiritual, physical, and personal blessings to His children. Further, He has provided us with written documentation of His bequest through the Old and New Testaments, or Covenants, of the Holy Bible.

By biblical standards, a covenant is an unbreakable contract that binds the instigator to meet the terms of the agreement, no matter whether the recipient performs according to the contract conditions or not. The greatest covenant gift God has bestowed on us is salvation and eternal life through the shed blood of His Son, Jesus Christ. Nothing we can do will earn us a position in the kingdom of God. The only way we can respond is simply to receive the blessing by faith.

Our heavenly Father has also made provision for each of us in all facets of our lives. In the following pages, you will find His unbreakable promises to you. Just as you received salvation by faith, accept these gifts that God offers to you. He offers them with the same motivation that He provided salvation for anyone who would believe—because He first loved us.

May you be abundantly blessed,
—The Publisher

📖 Bible Promises That God Will...

📖 FULFILL HIS PROMISES

Blessed be the Lord, that hath given rest unto his people Israel, according to all that he promised: there hath not failed one word of all his good promise.   1 Kings 8:56

I have spoken it, I will also bring it to pass; I have purposed it, I will also do it.   Isaiah 46:11

For he is faithful that promised.   Hebrews 10:23

According as his divine power hath given unto us all things that pertain unto life and godliness, through the knowledge of him that hath called us to glory and virtue: whereby are given unto us exceeding great and precious promises: that by these ye might be partakers of the divine nature.   2 Peter 1:3-4

11

God is not a man, that he should lie; neither the son of man, that he should repent: hath he said, and shall he not do it? or hath he spoken, and shall he not make it good?   Numbers 23:19

Know therefore that the Lord thy God, he is God, the faithful God, which keepeth covenant and mercy with them that love him and keep his commandments to a thousand generations.   Deuteronomy 7:9

Nevertheless my lovingkindness will I not utterly take from him, nor suffer my faithfulness to fail. My covenant will I not break, nor alter the thing that is gone out of my lips.   Psalm 89:33-34

Thy word is true from the beginning: and every one of thy righteous judgments endureth for ever.   Psalm 119:160

And, behold, I send the promise of my Father upon you: but tarry ye in the city of Jerusalem, until ye be endued with power from on high.   Luke 24:49

The Lord is not slack concerning his promise, as some men count slackness; but is longsuffering to us-ward.   2 Peter 3:9

That God Will...

For he remembered his holy promise, and Abraham his servant. And he brought forth his people with joy, and his chosen with gladness: And gave them the lands of the heathen: and they inherited the labor of the people; That they might observe his statutes, and keep his laws. Praise ye the LORD.   Psalm 105:42-45

And, being assembled together with them, commanded them that they should not depart from Jerusalem, but wait for the promise of the Father, which, saith he, ye have heard of me. For John truly baptized with water; but ye shall be baptized with the Holy Ghost not many days hence.   Acts 1:4-5

Therefore being by the right hand of God exalted, and having received of the Father the promise of the Holy Ghost, he hath shed forth this, which ye now see and hear.   Acts 2:33

For all the promises of God in him are yea, and in him Amen, unto the glory of God by us.   2 Corinthians 1:20

📖 HEAR OUR PRAYERS

He will regard the prayer of the destitute, and not despise their prayer.   Psalm 102:17

13

If my people, which are called by my name, shall humble themselves, and pray, and seek my face, and turn from their wicked ways; then will I hear from heaven, and will forgive their sin, and will heal their land.

2 Chronicles 7:14

If thou return to the Almighty, thou shalt be built up, thou shalt put away iniquity far from thy tabernacles...For then shalt thou have thy delight in the Almighty, and shalt lift up thy face unto God. Thou shalt make thy prayer unto him, and he shall hear thee.

Job 22:23, 26-27

But know that the LORD hath set apart him that is godly for himself: the LORD will hear when I call unto him.   Psalm 4:3

The righteous cry, and the LORD heareth, and delivereth them out of all their troubles.

Psalm 34:17

For the eyes of the Lord are over the righteous, and his ears are open unto their prayers.

1 Peter 3:12

This is the confidence that we have in him, that if we ask any thing according to his will, he heareth us.   1 John 5:14

That God Will...

📖 RESPOND TO OUR PRAYERS

Then shalt thou call, and the LORD shall answer; thou shalt cry, and he shall say, Here I am. Isaiah 58:9

And it shall come to pass, that before they call, I will answer; and while they are yet speaking, I will hear. Isaiah 65:24

Call unto me, and I will answer thee, and show thee great and mighty things, which thou knowest not. Jeremiah 33:3

Ask, and it shall be given you; seek, and ye shall find; knock, and it shall be opened unto you: For every one that asketh receiveth; and he that seeketh findeth; and to him that knocketh it shall be opened. Matthew 7:7-8

If two of you shall agree on earth as touching any thing that they shall ask, it shall be done for them of my Father which is in heaven. Matthew 18:19

Hitherto have ye asked nothing in my name: ask, and ye shall receive, that your joy may be full. John 16:24

If ye abide in me, and my words abide in you, ye shall ask what ye will, and it shall be done unto you. John 15:7

And if we know that he hear us, whatsoever we ask, we know that we have the petitions that we desired of him. 1 John 5:15

📖 Bible Promises Concerning...

📖 ABUNDANCE

For the LORD God is a sun and shield: the LORD will give grace and glory: no good thing will he withhold from them that walk uprightly.   Psalm 84:11

Seek ye first the kingdom of God, and his righteousness; and all these things shall be added unto you.   Matthew 6:33

My God shall supply all your needs according to his riches in glory by Christ Jesus.
                              Philippians 4:19

And Hezekiah had exceeding much riches and honor: and he made himself treasuries for silver, and for gold, and for precious stones, and for spices, and for shields, and for all manner of pleasant jewels; Storehouses also for the increase of corn, and wine, and oil; and stalls for all manner of beasts, and cotes for flocks. Moreover he provided him cities, and possessions of flocks and herds in abundance: for God had given him substance very much. 2 Chronicles 32:27-29

I [wisdom] love them that love me; and those that seek me early shall find me. Riches and honor are with me; yea, durable riches and righteousness. My fruit is better than gold, yea, than fine gold; and my revenue than choice silver. I lead in the way of righteousness, in the midst of the paths of judgment: That I may cause those that love me to inherit substance; and I will fill their treasures.

Proverbs 8:17-21

For all these things do the nations of the world seek after: and your Father knoweth that ye have need of these things. But rather seek ye the kingdom of God; and all these things shall be added unto you.

Luke 12:30-31

Concerning...

And it shall come to pass, if thou shalt hearken diligently unto the voice of the LORD thy God, to observe and to do all his commandments which I command thee this day...the LORD shall make thee plenteous in goods, in the fruit of thy body, and in the fruit of thy cattle, and in the fruit of thy ground, in the land which the LORD sware unto thy fathers to give thee. The LORD shall open unto thee his good treasure, the heaven to give the rain unto thy land in his season, and to bless all the work of thine hand: and thou shalt lend unto many nations, and thou shalt not borrow. And the LORD shall make thee the head, and not the tail; and thou shalt be above only, and thou shalt not be beneath; if that thou hearken unto the commandments of the LORD thy God, which I command thee this day, to observe and to do them.   Deuteronomy 28:1, 11-13

So the children went in and possessed the land...And they took strong cities, and a fat land, and possessed houses full of all goods, wells digged, vineyards, and oliveyards, and fruit trees in abundance: so they did eat, and were filled, and became fat, and delighted themselves in thy great goodness.
                    Nehemiah 9:24-25

O fear the LORD, ye his saints: for there is no want to them that fear him. The young lions do lack, and suffer hunger: but they that seek the LORD shall not want any good thing.

Psalm 34:9-10

But the meek shall inherit the earth; and shall delight themselves in the abundance of peace.

Psalm 37:11

📖 CHILDREN

He maketh the barren woman to keep house, and to be a joyful mother of children. Praise ye the LORD.

Psalm 113:9

Lo, children are an heritage of the LORD: and the fruit of the womb is his reward. As arrows are in the hand of a mighty man; so are children of the youth. Happy is the man that hath his quiver full of them.

Psalm 127:3-5

In the fear of the LORD is strong confidence: and his children shall have a place of refuge.

Proverbs 14:26

The just man walketh in his integrity: his children are blessed after him.

Proverbs 20:7

Concerning...

And ye shall serve the LORD your God, and he shall bless thy bread, and thy water...There shall nothing cast their young, nor be barren, in thy land.   Exodus 23:25-26

If ye hearken to these judgments, and keep, and do them, that the LORD thy God shall keep unto thee the covenant...he will love thee, and bless thee, and multiply thee: he will also bless the fruit of thy womb...there shall not be male or female barren among you.   Deuteronomy 7:12-14

Yet setteth he the poor on high from afflic- tion, and maketh him families like a flock.
                    Psalm 107:41

He will bless them that fear the LORD, both small and great. The LORD shall increase you more and more, you and your children.
                    Psalm 115:13-14

Thy wife shall be as a fruitful vine by the sides of thine house: thy children like olive plants round about thy table.   Psalm 128:3

Children's children are the crown of old men; and the glory of children are their fathers.
                    Proverbs 17:6

They send forth their little ones like a flock, and their children dance. Job 21:11

He hath blessed thy children within thee.
Psalm 147:13

The father of the righteous shall greatly rejoice: and he that begetteth a wise child shall have joy of him. Thy father and thy mother shall be glad, and she that bare thee shall rejoice. Proverbs 23:24-25

For I will pour water upon him that is thirsty, and floods upon the dry ground: I will pour my spirit upon thy seed, and my blessing upon thine offspring. Isaiah 44:3

And all thy children shall be taught of the LORD; and great shall be the peace of thy children. Isaiah 54:13

And I will give them one heart, and one way, that they may fear me for ever, for the good of them, and of their children after them.
Jeremiah 32:39

For the promise is unto you, and to your children, and to all that are afar off, even as many as the Lord our God shall call. Acts 2:39

Concerning...

📖 COMFORT

Yea, though I walk through the valley of the shadow of death, I will fear no evil: for thou art with me; thy rod and thy staff they comfort me.   Psalm 23:4

In the multitude of my thoughts within me thy comforts delight my soul.   Psalm 94:19

Remember the word unto thy servant, upon which thou hast caused me to hope. This is my comfort in my affliction: for thy word hath quickened me.   Psalm 119:49-50

Sing, O heavens; and be joyful, O earth; and break forth into singing, O mountains: for the LORD hath comforted his people, and will have mercy upon his afflicted.   Isaiah 49:13

I, even I, am he that comforteth you: who art thou, that thou shouldest be afraid of a man that shall die, and of the son of man which shall be made as grass.   Isaiah 51:12

And I will pray the Father, and he shall give you another Comforter, that he may abide with you for ever...I will not leave you comfortless: I will come to you.   John 14:16-18

Thou shalt increase my greatness, and comfort me on every side. Psalm 71:21

The spirit of the Lord GOD is upon me; because the LORD hath anointed me…to comfort all that mourn. Isaiah 61:2

Blessed are they that mourn: for they shall be comforted. Matthew 5:4

For whatsoever things were written aforetime were written for our learning, that we through patience and comfort of the scriptures might have hope. Romans 15:4

Blessed be God, even the Father of our Lord Jesus Christ, the Father of mercies, and the God of all comfort; who comforteth us in all our tribulation, that we may be able to comfort them which are in any trouble, by the comfort wherewith we ourselves are comforted of God. 2 Corinthians 1:3-4

Now our Lord Jesus Christ himself, and God, even our Father, which hath loved us, and hath given us everlasting consolation and good hope through grace, Comfort your hearts, and stablish you in every good word and work. 2 Thessalonians 2:16-17

Concerning...

This is my comfort in my affliction: for thy word hath quickened me. Psalm 119:50

For the LORD shall comfort Zion: he will comfort all her waste places; and he will make her wilderness like Eden, and her desert like the garden of the LORD; joy and gladness shall be found therein, thanksgiving, and the voice of melody. Isaiah 51:3

As one whom his mother comforteth, so will I comfort you; and ye shall be comforted in Jerusalem. Isaiah 66:13

For I will turn their mourning into joy, and will comfort them, and make them rejoice from their sorrow. Jeremiah 31:13

Thus saith the LORD of hosts; My cities through prosperity shall yet be spread abroad; and the LORD shall yet comfort Zion, and shall yet choose Jerusalem. Zechariah 1:17

If there be therefore any consolation in Christ, if any comfort of love, if any fellowship of the Spirit, if any bowels and mercies, Fulfill ye my joy, that ye be like-minded, having the same love, being of one accord, of one mind.
Philippians 2:1-2

I have seen his ways, and will heal him: I will lead him also, and restore comforts unto him.

Isaiah 57:18

But Jesus turned him about, and when he saw her, he said, Daughter, be of good comfort; thy faith hath made thee whole.   Matthew 9:22

Be perfect, be of good comfort, be of one mind, live in peace; and the God of love and peace shall be with you.   2 Corinthians 13:11

That their hearts might be comforted, being knit together in love, and unto all riches of the full assurance of understanding, to the acknowledgment of the mystery of God, and of the Father, and of Christ.   Colossians 2:2

📖 CONFIDENCE

For the LORD shall be thy confidence, and shall keep thy foot from being taken.

Proverbs 3:26

Being confident of this very thing, that he which hath begun a good work in you will perform it until the day of Jesus Christ.

Philippians 1:6

Concerning...

By terrible things in righteousness wilt thou answer us, O God of our salvation; who art the confidence of all the ends of the earth.

Psalm 65:5

For thus saith the Lord GOD, the Holy One of Israel; In returning and rest shall ye be saved; in quietness and in confidence shall be your strength.

Isaiah 30:15

And they shall dwell safely therein, and shall build houses, and plant vineyards; yea, they shall dwell with confidence, when I have executed judgments upon all those that despise them round about them; and they shall know that I am the LORD their God.

Ezekiel 28:26

This is the confidence that we have in him, that, if we ask any thing according to his will. he heareth us: And if we know that he hears us, whatsoever we ask, we know that we have the petitions that we desired of him.

1 John 5:14-15

Beloved, if our heart condemn us not, then have we confidence toward God. And whatsoever we ask, we receive of him, because we keep his commandments, and do those things that are pleasing in his sight.

1 John 3:21-22

In the fear of the LORD is strong confidence: and his children shall have a place of refuge.

Proverbs 14:26

In whom we have boldness and access with confidence by the faith of him.　Ephesians 3:12

📖 DELIVERANCE FROM EVIL

The angel of the LORD encampeth round about them that fear him, and delivereth them.　Psalm 34:7

The LORD shall preserve thee from all evil: he shall preserve thy soul.　Psalm 121:7

Who hath delivered us from the power of darkness, and hath translated us into the kingdom of his dear Son.　Colossians 1:13

And the Lord shall deliver me from every evil work, and will preserve me unto his heavenly kingdom: to whom be glory for ever and ever. Amen.　2 Timothy 4:18

We know that whosoever is born of God sinneth not; but he that is begotten of God keepeth himself, and that wicked one toucheth him not.　1 John 5:18

Concerning...

Ye that love the LORD, hate evil: he preserveth the souls of his saints; he delivereth them out of the hand of the wicked.   Psalm 97:10

Because thou hast made the LORD, which is my refuge, even the most High, thy habitation; There shall no evil befall thee, neither shall any plague come nigh thy dwelling. For he shall give his angels charge over thee, to keep thee in all thy ways.   Psalm 91:9-11

For I am persuaded, that neither death, nor life, nor angels, nor principalities, nor powers, nor things present, nor things to come, Nor height, nor depth, nor any other creature, shall be able to separate us from the love of God, which is in Christ Jesus our Lord.

Romans 8:38-39

But the Lord is faithful, who shall stablish you, and keep you from evil.   2 Thessalonians 3:3

ETERNAL LIFE

For God so loved the world, that he gave his only begotten Son, that whosoever believeth in him should not perish, but have everlasting life.   John 3:16

He that believeth on the Son hath everlasting life.   John 3:36

My sheep hear my voice, and I know them, and they follow me: And I give unto them eternal life; and they shall never perish.
                                    John 10:27-28

He that loveth his life shall lose it; and he that hateth his life in this world shall keep it unto life eternal.   John 12:25

But now being made free from sin, and become servants to God, ye have your fruit unto holiness, and the end everlasting life. For the wages of sin is death; but the gift of God is eternal life through Jesus Christ our Lord.
                                    Romans 6:22-23

In hope of eternal life, which God, that cannot lie, promised before the world began.
                                    Titus 1:2

This is the promise that he hath promised us, even eternal life.   1 John 2:25

These things have I written unto you that believe on the name of the Son of God; that ye may know that ye have eternal life. 1 John 5:13

Concerning...

Verily, verily, I say unto you, He that heareth my word, and believeth on him that sent me, hath everlasting life, and shall not come into condemnation; but is passed from death unto life.   John 5:24

And this is the record, that God hath given to us eternal life, and this life is in his Son. He that hath the Son hath life; and he that hath not the Son of God hath not life.

1 John 5:11-12

📖 FAMILY BLESSINGS

Lo, children are an heritage of the LORD: and the fruit of the womb is his reward.

Psalm 127:3

The house of the righteous shall stand.

Proverbs 12:7

And all thy children shall be taught of the LORD; and great shall be the peace of thy children.   Isaiah 54:13

And I will give them one heart, and one way, that they may fear me for ever, for the good of them, and of their children after them.

Jeremiah 32:39

Observe and hear all these words which I command thee, that it may go well with thee, and with thy children after thee for ever, when thou doest that which is good and right in the sight of the LORD thy God.   Deuteronomy 12:28

Blessed is the man that feareth the LORD, that delighteth greatly in his commandments. His seed shall be mighty upon earth: the generation of the upright shall be blessed.
Psalm 112:1-2

The LORD shall increase you more and more, you and your children.   Psalm 115:14

Thy wife shall be as a fruitful vine by the sides of thine house: thy children like olive plants round about thy table.   Psalm 128:3

He blesseth the habitation of the just.
Proverbs 3:33

The just man walketh in his integrity: his children are blessed after him.   Proverbs 20:7

For I will pour water upon him that is thirsty, and floods upon the dry ground: I will pour my spirit upon thy seed, and my blessing upon thine offspring.   Isaiah 44:3

Concerning...

Thou shalt keep therefore his statutes, and his commandments, which I command thee this day, that it may go well with thee, and with thy children after thee, and that thou mayest prolong thy days upon the earth, which the LORD thy God giveth thee, for ever.   Deuteronomy 4:40

And thou shalt rejoice in every good thing which the LORD thy God hath given unto thee, and unto thine house.   Deuteronomy 26:11

As arrows are in the hand of a mighty man; so are children of the youth. Happy is the man that hath his quiver full of them: they shall not be ashamed, but they shall speak with the enemies in the gate.   Psalm 127:4-5

Children's children are the crown of old men; and the glory of children are their fathers.
Proverbs 17:6

Train up a child in the way he should go: and when he is old, he will not depart from it.
Proverbs 22:6

Honor thy father and mother; which is the first commandment with promise; That it may be well with thee, and thou mayest live long on the earth.   Ephesians 6:2-3

On this wise ye shall bless the children of Is-rael, saying unto them: The LORD bless thee, and keep thee: The LORD make his face shine upon thee, and be gracious unto thee: The LORD lift up his countenance upon thee, and give thee peace. And they shall put my name upon the children of Israel; and I will bless them.   Numbers 6:23-27

And if it seem evil unto you to serve the LORD, choose you this day whom ye will serve; whether the gods which your fathers served that were on the other side of the flood, or the gods of the Amorites, in whose land ye dwell: but as for me and my house, we will serve the LORD.   Joshua 24:15

A good man leaveth an inheritance to his children's children: and the wealth of the sin-ner is laid up for the just.   Proverbs 13:22

And he shall turn the heart of the fathers to the children, and the heart of the children to their fathers, lest I come and smite the earth with a curse.   Malachi 4:6

And they said, Believe on the Lord Jesus Christ, and thou shalt be saved, and thy house.
                                                              Acts 16:31

Concerning...

The father of the righteous shall greatly rejoice: and he that begetteth a wise child shall have joy of him.   Proverbs 23:24

Correct thy son, and he shall give thee rest; yea, he shall give delight unto thy soul.
                                                                 Proverbs 29:17

Who can find a virtuous woman? for her price is far above rubies. The heart of her husband doth safely trust in her, so that he shall have no need of spoil....Her children arise up, and call her blessed; her husband also, and he praiseth her.   Proverbs 31:10-11, 28

📖 FAVOR

But the LORD was with Joseph, and showed him mercy, and gave him favor in the sight of the keeper of the prison.   Genesis 39:21

I will give this people favor in the sight of the Egyptians: and it shall come to pass, that, when ye go, ye shall not go empty.   Exodus 3:21

Of a truth I perceive that God is no respecter of persons: But in every nation he that feareth him, and worketh righteousness, is accepted with him.   Acts 10:34-35

And the LORD gave the people favor in the sight of the Egyptians, so that they lent unto them such things as they required. And they spoiled the Egyptians. Exodus 12:36

O Naphtali, satisfied with favor, and full with the blessing of the LORD: possess thou the west and the south. Deuteronomy 33:23

Then she said, Let me find favor in thy sight, my lord; for that thou hast comforted me, and for that thou hast spoken friendly unto thine handmaid, though I be not like unto one of thine handmaidens. Ruth 2:13

And the child Samuel grew on, and was in favor both with the LORD, and also with men. 1 Samuel 2:26

He shall pray unto God, and he will be favorable unto him: and he shall see his face with joy: for he will render unto man his righteousness. Job 33:26

For they got not the land in possession by their own sword, neither did their own arm save them: but thy right hand, and thine arm, and the light of thy countenance, because thou hadst a favor unto them. Psalm 44:3

Concerning...

Thou hast granted me life and favor, and thy visitation hath preserved my spirit.   Job 10:12

For thou, LORD, wilt bless the righteous; with favor wilt thou compass him as with a shield.
Psalm 5:12

For his anger endureth but a moment; in his favor is life: weeping may endure for a night, but joy cometh in the morning.   Psalm 30:5

But thou, O LORD, be merciful unto me, and raise me up, that I may requite them. By this I know that thou favorest me, because mine enemy doth not triumph over me And as for me, thou upholdest me in mine integrity, and settest me before thy face for ever.
Psalm 41:10-12

My son, forget not my law; but let thine heart keep my commandments...So shalt thou find favor and good understanding in the sight of God and man.   Proverbs 3:1, 4

He that diligently seeketh good procureth favor.   Proverbs 11:27

A good man obtaineth favor of the LORD.
Proverbs 12:2

For thou art the glory of their strength: and in thy favor our horn [power] shall be exalted.
Psalm 89:17

Remember me, O LORD, with the favor that thou bearest unto thy people: O visit me with thy salvation.
Psalm 106:4

I entreated thy favor with my whole heart: be merciful unto me according to thy word.
Psalm 119:58

For whoso findeth me findeth life, and shall obtain favor of the LORD.
Proverbs 8:35

Good understanding giveth favor.
Proverbs 13:15

Among the righteous there is favor.
Proverbs 14:9

The king's favor is toward a wise servant.
Proverbs 14:35

In the light of the king's countenance is life; and his favor is as a cloud of the latter rain.
Proverbs 16:15

Whoso findeth a wife findeth a good thing, and obtaineth favor of the LORD.
Proverbs 18:22

Concerning...

A good name is rather to be chosen than great riches, and loving favor rather than silver and gold.   Proverbs 22:1

Then was I in his eyes as one that found favor.
Song of Solomon 8:10

In my favor have I had mercy on thee.
Isaiah 60:10

Children in whom was no blemish, but well favored, and skillful in all wisdom, and cunning in knowledge, and understanding science, and such as had ability in them to stand in the king's palace, and whom they might teach the learning and the tongue of the Chaldeans.   Daniel 1:4

Now God had brought Daniel into favor and tender love with the prince of the eunuchs.
Daniel 1:9

And the patriarchs, moved with envy, sold Joseph into Egypt: but God was with him, And delivered him out of all his afflictions, and gave him favor and wisdom in the sight of Pharaoh king of Egypt; and he made him governor over Egypt and all his house.
Acts 7:9-10

And the angel came in unto her, and said, Hail, thou that art highly favored, the Lord is with thee: blessed art thou among women.... And the angel said unto her, Fear not, Mary: for thou hast found favor with God.

Luke 1:28, 30

And Jesus increased in wisdom and stature, and in favor with God and man.   Luke 2:52

And they, continuing daily with one accord in the temple, and breaking bread from house to house, did eat their meat with gladness and singleness of heart, Praising God, and having favor with all the people.   Acts 2:46-47

📖 FOOD

The God of Jacob...which made heaven, and earth, the sea, and all that therein is: which keepeth truth for ever: which executeth judgment for the oppressed: which giveth food to the hungry.   Psalm 146:5-7

Honor the LORD with thy substance, and with the firstfruits of all thine increase: so shall thy barns be filled with plenty, and thy presses shall burst out with new wine.   Proverbs 3:9-10

Concerning...

The LORD knoweth the days of the upright: and their inheritance shall be for ever. They shall not be ashamed in the evil time: and in the days of famine they shall be satisfied.

Psalm 37:18-19

I have been young, and now am old; yet have I not seen the righteous forsaken, nor his seed begging bread.   Psalm 37:25

He hath given meat unto them that fear him: he will ever be mindful of his covenant.

Psalm 111:5

Therefore I say unto you, Take no thought for your life, what ye shall eat, or what ye shall drink...Is not the life more than meat...? Behold the fowls of the air: for they sow not, neither do they reap, nor gather into barns; yet your heavenly Father feedeth them. Are ye not much better than they?...Therefore take no thought, saying, What shall we eat? or, What shall we drink?...(For after all these things do the Gentiles seek:) for your heavenly Father knoweth that ye have need of all these things. But seek ye first the kingdom of God, and his righteousness; and all these things shall be added unto you.

Matthew 6: 25-26, 31-33

For by them judgeth he the people; he giveth meat in abundance. Job 36:31

If ye be willing and obedient, ye shall eat the good of the land. Isaiah 1:19

📖 FORGIVENESS

Blessed is he whose transgression is forgiven, whose sin is covered. Blessed is the man unto whom the LORD imputeth not iniquity, and in whose spirit there is no guile. Psalm 32:1-2

I will put my law in their inward parts, and write it in their hearts; and will be their God, and they shall be my people...For I will forgive their iniquity, and I will remember their sin no more. Jeremiah 31:33-34

Who hath delivered us from the power of darkness, and hath translated us into the kingdom of his dear Son: in whom we have redemption through his blood, even the forgiveness of sins. Colossians 1:14

If we confess our sins, he is faithful and just to forgive us our sins, and to cleanse us from all unrighteousness. 1 John 1:9

Concerning...

If my people, which are called by my name, shall humble themselves, and pray, and seek my face, and turn from their wicked ways; then will I hear from heaven, and will forgive their sin, and will heal their land.

2 Chronicles 7:14

As far as the east is from the west, so far hath he removed our transgressions from us.

Psalm 103:12

But there is forgiveness with thee, that thou mayest be feared.   Psalm 130:4

I, even I, am he that blotteth out thy transgressions for mine own sake, and will not remember thy sins.   Isaiah 43:25

There is therefore now no condemnation to them which are in Christ Jesus, who walk not after the flesh, but after the Spirit.   Romans 8:1

In whom we have redemption through his blood, the forgiveness of sins, according to the riches of his grace.   Ephesians 1:7

I write unto you, little children, because your sins are forgiven you for his name's sake.

1 John 2:12

Thou hast forgiven the iniquity of thy people, thou hast covered all their sin.   Psalm 85:2

Come now, and let us reason together, saith the LORD: though your sins be as scarlet, they shall be as white as snow; though they be red like crimson, they shall be as wool.   Isaiah 1:18

And I will cleanse them from all their iniquity, whereby they have sinned against me; and I will pardon all their iniquities, whereby they have sinned, and whereby they have transgressed against me.   Jeremiah 33:8

To him give all the prophets witness, that through his name whosoever believeth in him shall receive remission of sins.   Acts 10:43

And you, being dead in your sins and the uncircumcision of your flesh, hath he quickened together with him, having forgiven you all trespasses.   Colossians 2:13

📖 FREEDOM

Now the Lord is that Spirit: and where the Spirit of the Lord is, there is liberty.

2 Corinthians 3:17

Concerning...

The spirit of the Lord GOD is upon me...he hath sent me to bind up the brokenhearted, to proclaim liberty to the captives, and the opening of the prison to them that are bound.

Isaiah 61:1

If the Son therefore shall make you free, ye shall be free indeed. John 8:36

For sin shall not have dominion over you: for ye are not under the law, but under grace.

Romans 6:14

But now being made free from sin, and become servants to God, ye have your fruit unto holiness, and the end everlasting life.

Romans 6:22

There is therefore now no condemnation to them which are in Christ Jesus, who walk not after the flesh, but after the Spirit. For the law of the Spirit of life in Christ Jesus hath made me free from the law of sin and death.

Romans 8:2

Stand fast therefore in the liberty wherewith Christ hath made us free, and be not entangled again with the yoke of bondage.

Galatians 5:1

📖 GOD'S PRESENCE

And he said, My presence shall go with thee, and I will give thee rest. Exodus 33:14

Fear not: for I am with thee. Isaiah 43:5

Thou wilt show me the path of life: in thy presence is fullness of joy. Psalm 16:11

Yea, though I walk through the valley of the shadow of death, I will fear no evil: for thou art with me. Psalm 23:4

Thou shalt hide them in the secret of thy presence. Psalm 31:20

Surely the righteous shall give thanks unto thy name: the upright shall dwell in thy presence.
Psalm 140:13

For where two or three are gathered together in my name, there am I in the midst of them.
Matthew 18:20

If ye love me, keep my commandments. And I will pray the Father, and he shall give you another Comforter, that he may abide with you for ever. John 14:15-16

Concerning...

And, lo, I am with you alway, even unto the end of the world. Matthew 28:20

Draw nigh to God, and he will draw nigh to you. James 4:8

Behold, I stand at the door, and knock: if any man hear my voice, and open the door, I will come in to him, and will sup with him, and he with me. Revelation 3:20

📖 GOD'S SPIRIT

And it shall come to pass afterward, that I will pour out my spirit upon all flesh; and your sons and your daughters shall prophesy, your old men shall dream dreams, your young men shall see visions. And also upon the servants and upon the handmaids in those days will I pour out my spirit. Joel 2:28-29

Behold, I will pour out my spirit unto you, I will make known my words unto you. Proverbs 1:23

For I will pour water upon him that is thirsty, and floods upon the dry ground: I will pour my spirit upon thy seed, and my blessing upon thine offspring. Isaiah 44:3

If ye then, being evil, know how to give good gifts unto your children: how much more shall your heavenly Father give the Holy Spirit to them that ask him?   Luke 11:13

And I will pray the Father, and he shall give you another Comforter, that he may abide with you for ever; even the Spirit of truth...ye know him; for he dwelleth with you, and shall be in you.   John 14:16-17

But when the Comforter is come, whom I will send unto you from the Father, even the Spirit of truth, which proceedeth from the Father, he shall testify of me.   John 15:26

Nevertheless I tell you the truth; It is expedient for you that I go away: for if I go not away, the Comforter will not come unto you; but if I depart, I will send him unto you.   John 16:7

But ye shall receive power, after that the Holy Ghost is come upon you: and ye shall be witnesses unto me...unto the uttermost part of the earth.   Acts 1:8

Because ye are sons, God hath sent forth the Spirit of his Son into your hearts, crying, Abba, Father.   Galatians 4:6

Concerning...

I [John the Baptist] indeed baptize you with water unto repentance: but he that cometh after me is mightier than I, whose shoes I am not worthy to bear: he shall baptize you with the Holy Ghost, and with fire.

Matthew 3:11

Then Peter said unto them, Repent, and be baptized every one of you in the name of Jesus Christ for the remission of sins, and ye shall receive the gift of the Holy Ghost. For the promise is unto you, and to your children, and to all that are afar off, even as many as the Lord our God shall call.   Acts 2:38-39

Hereby know we that we dwell in him, and he in us, because he hath given us of his Spirit.

1 John 4:13

📖 GOD'S WORD

It is written, Man shall not live by bread alone, but by every word that proceedeth out of the mouth of God.   Matthew 4:4

Now, brethren, I commend you to God, and to the word of his grace, which is able to build you up, and to give you an inheritance among all them which are sanctified.   Acts 20:32

The secret things belong unto the LORD our God: but those things which are revealed belong unto us and to our children for ever, that we may do all the words of this law.

Deuteronomy 29:29

Be ye mindful always of his covenant; the word which he commanded to a thousand generations.   1 Chronicles 16:15

The grass withereth, the flower fadeth: but the word of our God shall stand for ever.   Isaiah 40:8

So shall my word be that goeth forth out of my mouth: it shall not return unto me void, but it shall accomplish that which I please, and it shall prosper in the thing whereto I sent it.

Isaiah 55:11

Search the Scriptures; for in them ye think ye have eternal life: and they are they which testify of me.   John 5:39

For the word of God is quick, and powerful, and sharper than any two-edged sword, piercing even to the dividing asunder of soul and spirit, and of the joints and marrow, and is a discerner of the thoughts and intents of the heart.   Hebrews 4:12

Concerning...

For ever, O LORD, thy word is settled in heaven.   Psalm 119:89

Thy word is a lamp unto my feet, and a light unto my path.   Psalm 119:105

All Scripture is given by inspiration of God, and is profitable for doctrine, for reproof, for correction, for instruction in righteousness: that the man of God may be perfect, thoroughly furnished unto all good works.   2 Timothy 3:16-17

Being born again, not of corruptible seed, but of incorruptible, by the word of God, which liveth and abideth for ever...But the word of the Lord endureth for ever. And this is the word which by the gospel is preached unto you.   1 Peter 1:23, 25

📖 GUIDANCE

The LORD is my shepherd...he leadeth me in the paths of righteousness for his name's sake.
                    Psalm 23:1, 3

The steps of a good man are ordered by the LORD: and he delighteth in his way.
                    Psalm 37:23

Show me thy ways, O LORD; teach me thy paths. Lead me in thy truth, and teach me: for thou art the God of my salvation; on thee do I wait all the day....The meek will he guide in judgment: and the meek will he teach his way. All the paths of the LORD are mercy and truth unto such as keep his covenant and his testimonies.   Psalm 25:4-5, 9-10

For thou art my rock and my fortress; therefore for thy name's sake lead me, and guide me.   Psalm 31:3

I will instruct thee and teach thee in the way which thou shalt go: I will guide thee with mine eye.   Psalm 32:8

God is our God for ever and ever: he will be our guide even unto death.   Psalm 48:14

Trust in the LORD with all thine heart; and lean not unto thine own understanding. In all thy ways acknowledge him, and he shall direct thy paths.   Proverbs 3:5-6

Thine ear shall hear a word behind thee, saying, This is the way, walk ye in it, when ye turn to the right hand. and when ye turn to the left.   Isaiah 30:21

Concerning...

He keepeth the paths of judgment, and preserveth the way of his saints.   Proverbs 2:8

My son, keep thy father's commandment, and
forsake not the law of thy mother: Bind them
continually upon thine heart, and tie them
about thy neck. When thou goest, it shall lead
thee; when thou sleepest, it shall keep thee;
and when thou awakest, it shall talk with
thee. For the commandment is a lamp; and
the law is light.   Proverbs 6:20-23

And I will bring the blind by a way that they
knew not; I will lead them in paths that they
have not known: I will make darkness light
before them, and crooked things straight.
These things will I do unto them, and not forsake them.   Isaiah 42:16

They shall not hunger nor thirst;... for he that
hath mercy on them shall lead them, even by
the springs of water shall he guide them.
        Isaiah 49:10

And the LORD shall guide thee continually,
and satisfy thy soul in drought, and make fat
thy bones: and thou shalt be like a watered
garden, and like a spring of water, whose
waters fail not.   Isaiah 58:11

Thou shalt guide me with thy counsel, and afterward receive me to glory.　Psalm 73:24

If I take the wings of the morning, and dwell in the uttermost parts of the sea; even there shall thy hand lead me, and thy right hand shall hold me.　Psalm 139:9-10

I lead in the way of righteousness, in the midst of the paths of judgment: that I may cause those that love me to inherit substance; and I will fill their treasures.　Proverbs 8:20-21

He shall feed his flock like a shepherd: he shall gather the lambs with his arm, and carry them in his bosom, and shall gently lead those that are with young.　Isaiah 40:11

Through the tender mercy of our God; whereby the dayspring from on high hath visited us, to give light to them that sit in darkness and in the shadow of death, to guide our feet into the way of peace.　Luke 1:78-79

Howbeit when he, the Spirit of truth, is come, he will guide you into all truth: for he shall not speak of himself; but whatsoever he shall hear, that shall he speak: and he will show you things to come.　John 16:13

Concerning...

📖 HARVEST

While the earth remaineth, seedtime and harvest, and cold and heat, and summer and winter, and day and night shall not cease.

Genesis 8:22

If ye walk in my statutes, and keep my commandments, and do them; then I will give you rain in due season, and the land shall yield her increase, and the trees of the field shall yield their fruit. And your threshing shall reach unto the vintage, and the vintage shall reach unto the sowing time: and ye shall eat your bread to the full, and dwell in your land safely. Leviticus 26:3-5

If ye hearken to these judgments, and keep, and do them, that the LORD thy God shall keep unto thee the covenant...he will also bless the fruit of thy womb, and the fruit of thy land, thy corn, and thy wine, and thine oil, the increase of thy kine, and the flocks of thy sheep, in the land which he sware unto thy fathers to give thee. Deuteronomy 7:12-13

He causeth the grass to grow for the cattle, and herb for the service of man: that he may bring forth food out of the earth. Psalm 104:14

When thou cuttest down thine harvest in thy field, and hast forgot a sheaf in the field, thou shalt not go again to fetch it: it shall be for the stranger, for the fatherless, and for the widow: that the LORD thy God may bless thee in all the work of thine hands.

Deuteronomy 24:19

Then shall he give the rain of thy seed, that thou shalt sow the ground withal; and bread of the increase of the earth, and it shall be fat and plenteous: in that day shall thy cattle feed in large pastures. Isaiah 30:23

Let us now fear the LORD our God, that giveth rain, both the former and the latter, in his season: he reserveth unto us the appointed weeks of the harvest. Jeremiah 5:24

Ask ye of the LORD rain in the time of the latter rain; so the LORD shall make bright clouds, and give them showers of rain, to every one grass in the field. Zechariah 10:1

Then saith he unto his disciples, The harvest truly is plenteous, but the laborers are few; pray ye therefore the Lord of the harvest, that he will send forth laborers into his harvest.

Matthew 9:37-38

Concerning…

Also, O Judah, he hath set an harvest for thee.

Hosea 6:11

📖 HEALING

…I am the LORD that healeth thee.

Exodus 15:26

Bless the LORD, O my soul, and forget not all his benefits, who forgiveth all thine iniquities; who healeth all thy diseases.

Psalm 103:2-3

He was wounded for our transgressions, he was bruised for our iniquities: the chastisement of our peace was upon him; and with his stripes we are healed.

Isaiah 53:5

Heal me, O LORD, and I shall be healed; save me, and I shall be saved: for thou art my praise.

Jeremiah 17:14

But unto you that fear my name shall the Sun of righteousness arise with healing in his wings.

Malachi 4:2

And he received them, and spake unto them of the kingdom of God, and healed them that had need of healing.

Luke 9:11

And Jesus went about all Galilee, teaching in their synagogues, and preaching the gospel of the kingdom, and healing all manner of sickness and all manner of disease among the people.   Matthew 4:23

Confess your faults one to another, and pray one for another, that ye may be healed. The effectual fervent prayer of a righteous man availeth much.   James 5:16

Who his own self bare our sins in his own body on the tree, that we, being dead to sins, should live unto righteousness: by whose stripes ye were healed.   1 Peter 2:24

📖 HEALTH

Wherefore it shall come to pass, if ye hearken to these judgments, and keep, and do them… the LORD will take away from thee all sickness, and will put none of the evil diseases of Egypt…upon thee.   Deuteronomy 7:12, 15

God be merciful unto us, and bless us; and cause his face to shine upon us; that thy way may be known upon earth, thy saving health among all nations.   Psalm 67:1-2

Concerning...

There shall no evil befall thee, neither shall any plague come nigh thy dwelling.   Psalm 91:10

Fear the LORD, and depart from evil. It shall be health to thy navel, and marrow to thy bones.   Proverbs 3:7-8

Then shall thy light break forth as the morning, and thine health shall spring forth speedily: and thy righteousness shall go before thee; the glory of the LORD shall be thy reward.   Isaiah 58:8

For I will restore health unto thee, and I will heal thee of thy wounds, saith the LORD.
    Jeremiah 30:17

Behold, I will bring it health and cure, and I will cure them.   Jeremiah 33:6

Beloved, I wish above all things that thou mayest prosper and be in health, even as thy soul prospereth.   3 John 1:2

HEAVEN

Nevertheless we, according to his promise, look for new heavens and a new earth, wherein dwelleth righteousness.   2 Peter 3:13

Rejoice, and be exceeding glad: for great is your reward in heaven. Matthew 5:12

And Jesus said unto him, Verily I say unto thee, Today shalt thou be with me in paradise.
Luke 23:43

And I John saw the holy city, new Jerusalem, coming down from God out of heaven, prepared as a bride adorned for her husband. And I heard a great voice out of heaven saying, Behold, the tabernacle of God is with men, and he will dwell with them, and they shall be his people, and God himself shall be with them, and be their God. Revelation 21:3

To an inheritance incorruptible, and undefiled, and that fadeth not away, reserved in heaven for you, who are kept by the power of God through faith unto salvation ready to be revealed in the last time. 1 Peter 1:4-5

Wherefore the rather, brethren, give diligence to make your calling and election sure: for if ye do these things, ye shall never fall: For so an entrance shall be ministered unto you abundantly into the everlasting kingdom of our Lord and Savior Jesus Christ.
2 Peter 1:10-11

Concerning...

For the hope which is laid up for you in heaven. Colossians 1:5

For here have we no continuing city, but we seek one to come. Hebrews 13:14

HONOR

And the LORD hath avouched thee this day to be his peculiar people, as he hath promised thee, and that thou shouldest keep all his commandments; and to make thee high above all nations which he hath made, in praise, and in name, and in honor; and that thou mayest be an holy people unto the LORD thy God, as he hath spoken. Deuteronomy 26:18-19

Now the LORD saith, Be it far from me; for them that honor me I will honor.
1 Samuel 2:30

A gracious woman retaineth honor: and strong men retain riches. Proverbs 11:16

But glory, honor, and peace, to every man that worketh good, to the Jew first, and also to the Gentile: For there is no respect of persons with God. Romans 2:10-11

What is man, that thou art mindful of him? and the son of man, that thou visitest him? For thou hast made him a little lower than the angels, and hast crowned him with glory and honor.   Psalm 8:4-5

Because he hath set his love upon me, therefore will I deliver him: I will set him on high, because he hath known my name. He shall call upon me, and I will answer him: I will be with him in trouble; I will deliver him, and honor him.   Psalm 91:14-15

Happy is the man that findeth wisdom, and the man that getteth understanding...Length of days is in her right hand; and in her left hand riches and honor.   Proverbs 3:13, 16

I wisdom dwell with prudence, and find out knowledge of witty inventions...I love them that love me; and those that seek me early shall find me. Riches and honor are with me; yea, durable riches and righteousness.
                                    Proverbs 8:12, 17-18

Who can find a virtuous woman? for her price is far above rubies...Strength and honor are her clothing; and she shall rejoice in time to come.   Proverbs 31:10, 25

Concerning...

And God said to Solomon, Because this was in thine heart, and thou hast not asked riches, wealth, or honor, nor the life of thine enemies, neither yet hast asked long life; but hast asked wisdom and knowledge for thyself, that thou mayest judge my people, over whom I have made thee king: wisdom and knowledge is granted unto thee; and I will give thee riches, and wealth, and honor.

2 Chronicles 1:11-12

Blessed is the man that feareth the LORD.... His horn shall be exalted with honor.

Psalm 112:1, 9

Wisdom is the principal thing; therefore get wisdom: and with all thy getting get understanding. Exalt her, and she shall promote thee: she shall bring thee to honor, when thou dost embrace her.　　　Proverbs 4:7-8

The fear of the LORD is the instruction of wisdom; and before honor is humility.

Proverbs 15:33

If any man serve me, let him follow me; and where I am, there shall also my servant be: if any man serve me, him will my Father honor.

John 12:26

Poverty and shame shall be to him that refuseth instruction: but he that regardeth reproof shall be honored. Proverbs 13:18

He that followeth after righteousness and
mercy findeth life, righteousness, and honor.
Proverbs 21:21

A man's pride shall bring him low: but honor
shall uphold the humble in spirit. Proverbs 29:23

📖 HOPE

Now the God of hope fill you with all joy and
peace in believing, that ye may abound in
hope, through the power of the Holy Ghost.
Romans 15:13

The eyes of your understanding being enlight-
ened; that ye may know what is the hope of
his calling, and what the riches of the glory of
his inheritance in the saints. Ephesians 1:18

For the hope which is laid up for you in
heaven, whereof ye heard before in the word
of the truth of the gospel. Colossians 1:5

Christ in you, the hope of glory.
Colossians 1:27

Concerning...

Be of good courage, and he shall strengthen your heart, all ye that hope in the LORD.

Psalm 31:24

By whom also we...rejoice in hope of the glory of God. And hope maketh not ashamed; because the love of God is shed abroad in our hearts by the Holy Ghost which is given unto us.

Romans 5:2, 5

For whatsoever things were written aforetime were written for our learning, that we through patience and comfort of the scriptures might have hope.

Romans 15:4

That by two immutable things, in which it was impossible for God to lie, we might have a strong consolation, who have fled for refuge to lay hold upon the hope set before us: Which hope we have as an anchor of the soul, both sure and stedfast, and which entereth into that within the veil.

Hebrews 6:18-19

Blessed be the God and Father of our Lord Jesus Christ, which according to his abundant mercy hath begotten us again unto a lively hope by the resurrection of Jesus Christ from the dead.

1 Peter 1:3

For thou art my hope, O Lord GOD: thou art my trust from my youth. Psalm 71:5

📖 INSTRUCTION

What man is he that feareth the LORD? him shall he teach in the way that he shall choose.
Psalm 25:12

I will instruct thee and teach thee in the way which thou shalt go: I will guide thee with mine eye. Psalm 32:8

He that refuseth instruction despiseth his own soul: but he that heareth reproof getteth understanding. The fear of the LORD is the instruction of wisdom, and before honor is humility. Proverbs 15:32-33

Hear counsel, and receive instruction, that thou mayest be wise in thy latter end. There are many devices in a man's heart; nevertheless the counsel of the LORD, that shall stand.
Proverbs 19:20-21

For his God doth instruct him to discretion, and doth teach him...This also cometh forth from the LORD of hosts, which is wonderful in counsel. Isaiah 28:26, 29

Concerning...

The fear of the LORD is the beginning of knowledge: but fools despise wisdom and instruction. My son, hear the instruction of thy father, and forsake not the law of thy mother: For they shall be an ornament of grace unto thy head, and chains about thy neck.

Proverbs 1:7-9

Receive my instruction, and not silver; and knowledge rather than choice gold. For wisdom is better than rubies; and all the things that may be desired are not to be compared to it...Counsel is mine, and sound wisdom: I am understanding; I have strength.

Proverbs 8:10-11, 14

Hear instruction, and be wise, and refuse it not. Blessed is the man that heareth me, watching daily at my gates, waiting at the posts of my doors. For whoso findeth me findeth life, and shall obtain favor of the LORD.

Proverbs 8:33-35

All scripture is given by inspiration of God, and is profitable for doctrine, for reproof, for correction, for instruction in righteousness: That the man of God may be perfect, thoroughly furnished unto all good works.

2 Timothy 3:16-17

Good and upright is the LORD: therefore will he teach sinners in the way. The meek will he guide in judgment and…will he teach his way.

Psalm 25:8-9

The counsel of the LORD standeth for ever, the thoughts of his heart to all generations.

Psalm 33:11

Thou shalt guide me with thy counsel, and afterward receive me to glory.　　Psalm 73:24

To know wisdom and instruction; to perceive the words of understanding; To receive the instruction of wisdom, justice, and judgment, and equity; To give subtlety to the simple, to the young man knowledge and discretion; A wise man will hear, and will increase learning; and a man of understanding shall attain unto wise counsels.　　Proverbs 1:2-5

Take fast hold of instruction; let her not go: keep her; for she is thy life.　　Proverbs 4:13

Give instruction to a wise man, and he will be yet wiser: teach a just man, and he will increase in learning. The fear of the LORD is the beginning of wisdom: and the knowledge of the holy is understanding.　　Proverbs 9:9-10

Concerning...

Understanding is a wellspring of life unto him that hath it: but the instruction of fools is folly. The heart of the wise teacheth his mouth, and addeth learning to his lips.   Proverbs 16:22-23

Come ye, and let us go up to the mountain of the LORD, to the house of the God of Jacob; and he will teach us of his ways, and we will walk in his paths: for out of Zion shall go forth the law, and the word of the LORD from Jerusalem.   Isaiah 2:3

But the Comforter, which is the Holy Ghost, whom the Father will send in my name, he shall teach you all things, and bring all things to your remembrance, whatsoever I have said unto you.   John 14:26

But the anointing which ye have received of him abideth in you, and ye need not that any man teach you: but as the same anointing teacheth you of all things, and is truth, and is no lie, and even as it hath taught you, ye shall abide in him.   1 John 2:27

Jesus' Return

Behold, he cometh with clouds; and every eye shall see him.   Revelation 1:7

For as the lightning cometh out of the east, and shineth even unto the west; so shall also the coming of the Son of man be…And then shall appear the sign of the Son of man in heaven: and then shall all the tribes of the earth mourn, and they shall see the Son of man coming in the clouds of heaven with power and great glory.　　　Matthew 24:27, 30

When Christ, who is our life, shall appear, then shall ye also appear with him in glory.
　　　　　　　　　　Colossians 3:4

For the Lord himself shall descend from heaven with a shout, with the voice of the archangel, and with the trump of God: and the dead in Christ shall rise first: Then we which are alive and remain shall be caught up together with them in the clouds, to meet the Lord in the air: and so shall we ever be with the Lord.　　　　1 Thessalonians 4:16-17

Looking for that blessed hope, and the glorious appearing of the great God and our Savior Jesus Christ.　　　　　　　Titus 2:13

Unto them that look for him shall he appear the second time without sin unto salvation.
　　　　　　　　　　Hebrews 9:28

Concerning...

For I know that my redeemer liveth, and that he shall stand at the latter day upon the earth.
Job 19:25

And Jesus said, I am: and ye shall see the Son of man sitting on the right hand of power, and coming in the clouds of heaven.   Mark 14:62

Blessed are those servants, whom the Lord when he cometh shall find watching.   Luke 12:37

In my Father's house are many mansions: if it were not so, I would have told you. I go to prepare a place for you. And if I go and prepare a place for you, I will come again, and receive you unto myself; that where I am, there ye may also be.   John 14:2-3

This same Jesus, which is taken up from you into heaven, shall so come in like manner as ye have seen him go into heaven.   Acts 1:11

For as often as ye eat this bread, and drink this cup, ye do show the Lord's death till he come.
1 Corinthians 11:26

But we know that, when he shall appear, we shall be like him; for we shall see him as he is.
1 John 3:2

Ye have heard how I said unto you, I said unto you, I go away, and come again unto you. If ye loved me, ye would rejoice, because I said, I go unto the Father.   John 14:28

📖 JOY

Thou wilt show me the path of life: in thy presence is fullness of joy; at thy right hand there are pleasures for evermore.   Psalm 16:11

They that sow in tears shall reap in joy. He that goeth forth and weepeth, bearing precious seed, shall doubtless come again with rejoicing, bringing his sheaves with him.
                                        Psalm 126:5-6

And the ransomed of the LORD shall return, and come to Zion with songs and everlasting joy upon their heads: they shall obtain joy and gladness, and sorrow and sighing shall flee away .   Isaiah 35:10

For ye shall go out with joy, and be led forth with peace: the mountains and the hills shall break forth before you into singing, and all the trees of the field shall clap their hands.
                                        Isaiah 55:12

Concerning...

For God giveth to a man that is good in his sight wisdom, and knowledge, and joy.

Ecclesiastes 2:26

The LORD thy God in the midst of thee is mighty; he will save, he will rejoice over thee with joy; he will rest in his love, he will joy over thee with singing.   Zephaniah 3:17

And the angel said unto them, Fear not: for, behold, I bring you good tidings of great joy, which shall be to all people.   Luke 2:10

These things have I spoken unto you, that my joy might remain in you, and that your joy might be full.   John 15:11

I will see you again, and your heart shall rejoice, and your joy no man taketh from you.

John 16:22

For the kingdom of God is not meat and drink; but righteousness, and peace, and joy in the Holy Ghost.   Romans 14:17

Whom having not seen, ye love; in whom, though now ye see him not, yet believing, ye rejoice with joy unspeakable and full of glory.

1 Peter 1:8

Go your way, eat the fat, and drink the sweet, and send portions unto them for whom nothing is prepared: for this day is holy unto our Lord: neither be ye sorry; for the joy of the LORD is your strength.   Nehemiah 8:10

I will greatly rejoice in the LORD, my soul shall be joyful in my God; for he hath clothed me with the garments of salvation, he hath covered me with the robe of righteousness, as a bridegroom decketh himself with ornaments, and as a bride adorneth herself with her jewels.   Isaiah 61:10

Yet I will rejoice in the LORD, I will joy in the God of my salvation.   Habakkuk 3:18

📖 LIFE AFTER DEATH

But if the Spirit of him that raised up Jesus from the dead dwell in you, he that raised up Christ from the dead shall also quicken your mortal bodies by his Spirit that dwelleth in you.   Romans 8:11

Knowing that he which raised up the Lord Jesus shall raise up us also by Jesus, and shall present us with you.   2 Corinthians 4:14

Concerning...

Jesus said unto her, I am the resurrection, and the life: he that believeth in me, though he were dead, yet shall he live: and whosoever liveth and believeth in me shall never die.

John 11:25-26

In a moment, in the twinkling of an eye, at the last trump: for the trumpet shall sound, and the dead shall be raised incorruptible, and we shall be changed. For this corruptible must put on incorruption, and this mortal must put on immortality.

1 Corinthians 15:52-53

For if we believe that Jesus died and rose again, even so them also which sleep in Jesus will God bring with him.

1 Thessalonians 4:14

Therefore are they before the throne of God, and serve him day and night in his temple: and he that sitteth on the throne shall dwell among them. They shall hunger no more, neither thirst any more; neither shall the sun light on them, nor any heat. For the Lamb which is in the midst of the throne shall feed them, and shall lead them unto living fountains of waters: and God shall wipe away all tears from their eyes.

Revelation 7:15-17

📖 LONGEVITY

That thou mightest fear the LORD thy God, to keep all his statutes and his commandments, which I command thee, thou, and thy son, and thy son's son, all the days of thy life; and that thy days may be prolonged.   Deuteronomy 6:2

Because he hath set his love upon me...With long life will I satisfy him, and show him my salvation.   Psalm 91:14, 16

Forget not my law; but let thine heart keep my commandments: For length of days, and long life, and peace, shall they add to thee.
                                        Proverbs 3:1-2

Exalt her [wisdom], and she shall promote thee...and the years of thy life shall be many.
                                        Proverbs 4:8, 10

The fear of the LORD is the beginning of wisdom...For by me thy days shall be multiplied, and the years of thy life shall be increased.
                                        Proverbs 9:10-11

The fear of the LORD prolongeth days: but the years of the wicked shall be shortened.
                                        Proverbs 10:27

Honor thy father and thy mother: that thy days may be long upon the land which the LORD thy God giveth thee. Exodus 20:12

Ye shall walk in all the ways which the LORD your God hath commanded you, that ye may live, and that it may be well with you, and that ye may prolong your days in the land which ye shall possess. Deuteronomy 5:33

Honor thy father and mother; which is the first commandment with promise; That it may be well with thee, and thou mayest live long on the earth. Ephesians 6:2-3

LOVE

For God so loved the world, that he gave his only begotten Son, that whosoever believeth in him should not perish, but have everlasting life. John 3:16

In this was manifested the love of God toward us, because that God sent his only begotten Son into the world, that we might live through him. Herein is love, not that we loved God, but that he loved us, and sent his Son to be the propitiation for our sins. 1 John 4:9-10

And he will love thee, and bless thee, and multiply thee.   Deuteronomy 7:13

The LORD hath appeared of old unto me, saying, Yea, I have loved thee with an everlasting love: therefore with lovingkindness have I drawn thee.   Jeremiah 31:3

As the Father hath loved me, so have I loved you: continue ye in my love.   John 15:9

For I am persuaded, that neither death, nor life, nor angels, nor principalities, nor powers, nor things present, nor things to come, Nor height, nor depth, nor any other creature, shall be able to separate us from the love of God, which is in Christ Jesus our Lord.
                    Romans 8:38-39

Behold, what manner of love the Father hath bestowed upon us, that we should be called the sons of God: therefore the world knoweth us not, because it knew him not.   1 John 3:1

And we have known and believed the love that God hath to us. God is love; and he that dwelleth in love dwelleth in God, and God in him…We love him, because he first loved us.
                    1 John 4:16, 19

Concerning...

He that loveth me shall be loved of my Father, and I will love him, and will manifest myself to him. John 14:21

For the Father himself loveth you, because ye have loved me, and have believed that I came out from God. John 16:27

But God commendeth his love toward us, in that, while we were yet sinners, Christ died for us. Romans 5:8

That Christ may dwell in your hearts by faith; that ye, being rooted and grounded in love, May be able to comprehend with all saints what is the breadth, and length, and depth, and height; And to know the love of Christ, which passeth knowledge, that ye might be filled with all the fullness of God.
Ephesians 3:17-19

📖 NEW LIFE

Therefore we are buried with him by baptism into death: that like as Christ was raised up from the dead by the glory of the Father, even so we also should walk in newness of life.
Romans 6:4

A new heart also will I give you, and a new spirit will I put within you: and I will take away the stony heart out of your flesh, and I will give you an heart of flesh.   Ezekiel 36:26

But we all, with open face beholding as in a glass the glory of the Lord, are changed into the same image from glory to glory, even as by the Spirit of the Lord.   2 Corinthians 3:18

Therefore if any man be in Christ, he is a new creature: old things are passed away; behold, all things are become new.

2 Corinthians 5:17

I am crucified with Christ: nevertheless I live; yet not I, but Christ liveth in me: and the life which I now live in the flesh I live by the faith of the Son of God, who loved me, and gave himself for me.   Galatians 2:20

Who his own self bare our sins in his own body on the tree, that we, being dead to sins, should live unto righteousness.   1 Peter 2:24

Whosoever is born of God doth not commit sin; for his seed remaineth in him: and he cannot sin, because he is born of God.

1 John 3:9

Concerning...

📖 PEACE

The LORD will bless his people with peace.
Psalm 29:11

But the meek shall inherit the earth; and shall delight themselves in the abundance of peace.
Psalm 37:11

He will speak peace unto his people, and to his saints: but let them not turn again to folly.
Psalm 85:8

Thou wilt keep him in perfect peace, whose mind is stayed on thee: because he trusteth in thee.
Isaiah 26:3

Peace I leave with you, my peace I give unto you: not as the world giveth, give I unto you. Let not your heart be troubled, neither let it be afraid.
John 14:27

Therefore being justified by faith, we have peace with God through our Lord Jesus Christ.
Romans 5:1

And the peace of God, which passeth all understanding, shall keep your hearts and minds through Christ Jesus.
Philippians 4:7

Great peace have they which love thy law: and nothing shall offend them. Psalm 119:165

When a man's ways please the LORD, he maketh even his enemies to be at peace with him.   Proverbs 16:7

LORD, thou wilt ordain peace for us.
                                        Isaiah 26:12

And the work of righteousness shall be peace; and the effect of righteousness quietness and assurance for ever.   Isaiah 32:17

But he was wounded for our transgressions, he was bruised for our iniquities: the chastisement of our peace was upon him; and with his stripes we are healed.   Isaiah 53:5

To be spiritually minded is life and peace.
                                        Romans 8:6

For he is our peace, who hath made both one, and hath broken down the middle wall of partition between us; Having abolished in his flesh the enmity, even the law of commandments contained in ordinances; for to make in himself of twain one new man, so making peace.   Ephesians 2:15

Concerning...

📖 PROSPERITY

Keep therefore the words of this covenant, and do them, that ye may prosper in all that ye do.
Deuteronomy 29:9

Believe in the Lord your God, so shall ye be established; believe his prophets, so shall ye prosper.
2 Chronicles 20:20

Only be thou strong and very courageous, that thou mayest observe to do according to all the law...turn not from it to the right hand or to the left, that thou mayest prosper whithersoever thou goest. This book of the law shall not depart out of thy mouth; but thou shalt meditate therein day and night, that thou mayest observe to do according to all that is written therein: for then thou shalt make thy way prosperous, and then thou shalt have good success.
Joshua 1:7-8

If they obey and serve him, they shall spend their days in prosperity, and their years in pleasures.
Job 36:11

I, even I, have spoken; yea, I have called him: I have brought him, and he shall make his way prosperous.
Isaiah 48:15

But thou shalt remember the LORD thy God: for it is he that giveth thee power to get wealth, that he may establish his covenant which he sware unto thy fathers, as it is this day.   Deuteronomy 8:18

Blessed is the man that walketh not in the counsel of the ungodly...But his delight is the law of the Lord; and in his law doth he meditate day and night. And he shall be like a tree planted by the rivers of water, that bringeth forth his fruit in his season; his leaf also shall not wither; and whatsoever he doeth shall prosper.   Psalm 1:1-3

For the seed shall be prosperous; the vine shall give her fruit, and the ground shall give her increase, and the heavens shall give their dew; and I will cause the remnant of this people to possess all these things. And it shall come to pass, that as ye were a curse among the heathen, O house of Judah, and house of Israel; so will I save you, and ye shall be a blessing: fear not, but let your hands be strong.
                    Zechariah 8:12-13

Beloved, I wish above all things that thou mayest prosper and be in health, even as thy soul prospereth.   3 John 2

Concerning...

Let the LORD be magnified, which hath pleasure in the prosperity of his servant.   Psalm 35:27

Pray for the peace of Jerusalem: they shall prosper that love thee. Peace be within thy walls, and prosperity within thy palaces.
Psalm 122:6-7

Behold, I will bring it health and cure, and I will cure them, and will reveal unto them the abundance of peace and truth...And it shall be to me a name of joy, a praise and an honor before all the nations of the earth, which shall hear all the good that I do unto them: and they shall fear and tremble for all the goodness and for all the prosperity that I procure unto it.
Jeremiah 33:6, 9

☐ PROTECTION

For the LORD God is a sun and shield: the LORD will give grace and glory: no good thing will he withhold from them that walk uprightly.   Psalm 84:11

For he shall give his angels charge over thee, to keep thee in all thy ways. They shall bear thee up in their hands, lest thou dash thy foot against a stone.   Psalm 91:11-12

He will keep the feet of his saints, and the wicked shall be silent in darkness; for by strength shall no man prevail.   1 Samuel 2:9

The LORD is my rock, and my fortress, and my deliverer; my God, my strength, in whom I will trust; my buckler, and the horn of my salvation, and my high tower.   Psalm 18:2

For who is God save the LORD? or who is a rock save our God? It is God that girdeth me with strength, and maketh my way perfect.
                              Psalm 18:31-32

O love the LORD, all ye his saints: for the LORD preserveth the faithful.   Psalm 31:23

Surely he shall deliver thee from the snare of the fowler, and from the noisome pestilence. He shall cover thee with his feathers, and under his wings shalt thou trust: his truth shall be thy shield and buckler.   Psalm 91:3-4

They that trust in the LORD shall be as mount Zion, which cannot be removed, but abideth for ever. As the mountains are round about Jerusalem, so the LORD is round about his people from henceforth even for ever.
                              Psalm 125:1-2

Concerning...

For thou, LORD, wilt bless the righteous; with favor wilt thou compass him as with a shield.

Psalm 5:12

Many are the afflictions of the righteous: but the LORD delivereth him out of them all.

Psalm 34:19

The LORD is thy keeper: the LORD is thy shade upon thy right hand. The sun shall not smite thee by day, nor the moon by night. The LORD shall preserve thee from all evil: he shall preserve thy soul. The LORD shall preserve thy going out and thy coming in from this time forth, and even for evermore.

Psalm 121:5-8

Every word of God is pure: he is a shield unto them that put their trust in him.

Proverbs 30:5

📖 RIGHTEOUSNESS

For with the heart man believeth unto righteousness; and with the mouth confession is made unto salvation.   Romans 10:10

For the fruit of the Spirit is in all goodness and righteousness and truth.   Ephesians 5:9

Now the righteousness of God without the law is manifested…Even the righteousness of God which is by faith of Jesus Christ unto all and upon all them that believe.　　Romans 3:21-22

Now to him that worketh is the reward not reckoned of grace, but of debt. But to him that worketh not, but believeth on him that justifieth the ungodly, his faith is counted for righteousness.　　Romans 4:4-5

For if by one man's offense death reigned by one; much more they which receive abundance of grace and of the gift of righteousness shall reign in life by one, Jesus Christ.
Romans 5:17

And if Christ be in you…the Spirit is life because of righteousness.　　Romans 8:10

But of him [God] are ye in Christ Jesus, who of God is made unto us wisdom, and righteousness, and sanctification, and redemption.
1 Corinthians 1:30

For he hath made him to be sin for us, who knew no sin; that we might be made the righteousness of God in him.
2 Corinthians 5:21

And be found in him, not having mine own righteousness, which is of the law, but that which is through the faith of Christ, the righteousness which is of God by faith.

Philippians 3:9

📖 SAFETY

Wherefore ye shall do my statutes, and keep my judgments, and do them; and ye shall dwell in the land in safety. Leviticus 25:18

The beloved of the LORD shall dwell in safety by him; and the LORD shall cover him all the day long, and he shall dwell between his shoulders. Deuteronomy 33:12

The God of my rock; in him will I trust: he is my shield, and the horn of my salvation, my high tower, and my refuge, my savior; thou savest me from violence. 2 Samuel 22:3

I will both lay me down in peace, and sleep: for thou, LORD, only makest me dwell in safety. Psalm 4:8

Where no counsel is, the people fall: but in the multitude of counselors there is safety.

Proverbs 11:14

If thou prepare thine heart, and stretch out thine hands toward him...thou shalt be secure, because there is hope; yea, thou shalt dig about thee, and thou shalt take thy rest in safety. Job 11:13, 18

For the oppression of the poor, for the sighing of the needy, now will I arise, saith the LORD; I will set him in safety from him that puffeth at him. Psalm 12:5

He that dwelleth in the secret place of the most High shall abide under the shadow of the Almighty. I will say of the LORD, He is my refuge and my fortress: my God; in him will I trust. Psalm 91:1-2

Though I walk in the midst of trouble, thou wilt revive me: thou shalt stretch forth thine hand against the wrath of mine enemies, and thy right hand shall save me. Psalm 138:7

The name of the LORD is a strong tower: the righteous runneth into it, and is safe.
Proverbs 18:10

The fear of man bringeth a snare: but whoso putteth his trust in the LORD shall be safe.
Proverbs 29:25

Concerning...

📖 SALVATION

For the LORD taketh pleasure in his people: he will beautify the meek with salvation.

Psalm 149:4

And she shall bring forth a son, and thou shalt call his name JESUS: for he shall save his people from their sins.   Matthew 1:21

For God sent not his Son into the world to condemn the world; but that the world through him might be saved.   John 3:17

If thou shalt confess with thy mouth the Lord Jesus, and shalt believe in thine heart that God hath raised him from the dead, thou shalt be saved. For with the heart man believeth unto righteousness; and with the mouth confession is made unto salvation.

Romans 10:9-10

For whosoever shall call upon the name of the Lord shall be saved.   Romans 10:13

For this is good and acceptable in the sight of God our Savior; who will have all men to be saved, and to come unto the knowledge of the truth.   1 Timothy 2:3-4

With long life will I satisfy him, and show him my salvation. Psalm 91:16

I am the door: by me if any man enter in, he shall be saved, and shall go in and out, and find pasture. John 10:9

And they said, Believe on the Lord Jesus Christ, and thou shalt be saved, and thy house. Acts 16:31

For if, when we were enemies, we were reconciled to God by the death of his Son, much more, being reconciled, we shall be saved by his life. Romans 5:10

In whom ye also trusted, after that ye heard the word of truth, the gospel of your salvation: in whom also after that ye believed, ye were sealed with that holy Spirit of promise. Ephesians 1:13

For by grace are ye saved through faith; and that not of yourselves: it is the gift of God: Not of works, lest any man should boast. Ephesians 2:8-9

For God hath not appointed us to wrath, but to obtain salvation by our Lord Jesus Christ. 1 Thessalonians 5:9

Concerning...

Not by works of righteousness which we have done, but according to his mercy he saved us, by the washing of regeneration, and renewing of the Holy Ghost; Which he shed on us abundantly through Jesus Christ our Savior; That being justified by his grace, we should be made heirs according to the hope of eternal life.   Titus 3:5-7

📖 SATISFACTION

With long life will I satisfy him, and show him my salvation.   Psalm 91:16

The fear of the LORD tendeth to life: and he that hath it shall abide satisfied; he shall not be visited with evil.   Proverbs 19:23

And I will satiate the soul of the priests with fatness, and my people shall be satisfied with my goodness, saith the LORD.   Jeremiah 31:14

Behold, I will send you corn, and wine, and oil, and ye shall be satisfied therewith...And ye shall eat in plenty, and be satisfied, and praise the name of the LORD your God, that hath dealt wondrously with you: and my people shall never be ashamed.   Joel 2:19, 26

A man shall be satisfied with good by the fruit of his mouth: and the recompense of a man's hands shall be rendered unto him.

Proverbs 12:14

Ho, every one that thirsteth, come ye to the waters, and he that hath no money; come ye, buy, and eat; yea, come, buy wine and milk without money and without price. Wherefore do ye spend money for that which is not bread? and your labor for that which satisfieth not? hearken diligently unto me, and eat ye that which is good, and let your soul delight itself in fatness. Incline your ear, and come unto me: hear, and your soul shall live; and I will make an everlasting covenant with you, even the sure mercies of David.

Isaiah 55:1-3

The LORD shall guide thee continually, and satisfy thy soul in drought, and make fat thy bones: and thou shalt be like a watered garden, and like a spring of water, whose waters fail not.

Isaiah 58:11

And Jesus said unto them, I am the bread of life: he that cometh to me shall never hunger; and he that believeth on me shall never thirst.

John 6:35

The meek shall eat and be satisfied: they shall praise the LORD that seek him: your heart shall live for ever. Psalm 22:26

How excellent is thy lovingkindness, O God! therefore the children of men put their trust under the shadow of thy wings. They shall be abundantly satisfied with the fatness of thy house; and thou shalt make them drink of the river of thy pleasures. Psalm 36:7-8

Who satisfieth thy mouth with good things; so that thy youth is renewed like the eagle's. Psalm 103:5

Oh that men would praise the LORD for his goodness, and for his wonderful works to the children of men! For he satisfieth the longing soul, and filleth the hungry soul with goodness. Psalm 107:8-9

Be content with such things as ye have: for he hath said, I will never leave thee, nor forsake thee. Hebrews 13:5

📖 SPIRITUAL GIFTS

For the gifts and calling of God are without repentance. Romans 11:29

I have filled him with the spirit of God, in wisdom, and in understanding, and in knowledge, and in all manner of workmanship, To devise cunning works, to work in gold, and in silver, and in brass, And in cutting of stones, to set them, and in carving of timber, to work in all manner of workmanship.   Exodus 31:3-5

If ye then, being evil, know how to give good gifts unto your children: how much more shall your heavenly Father give the Holy Spirit to them that ask him?   Luke 11:13

So we, being many, are one body in Christ, and every one members one of another. Having then gifts differing according to the grace that is given to us, whether prophecy...ministry...teaching...exhortation, or he that giveth...ruleth...[or] showeth mercy.
                    Romans 12:5-8

So that ye come behind in no gift; waiting for the coming of our Lord Jesus Christ.
                    1 Corinthians 1:7

Even so ye, forasmuch as ye are zealous of spiritual gifts, seek that ye may excel to the edifying of the church.   1 Corinthians 14:12

Concerning...

Now concerning spiritual gifts....there are diversities of gifts, but the same Spirit. And there are differences of administrations, but the same Lord. And there are diversities of operations, but it is the same God which worketh all in all. But the manifestation of the Spirit is given to every man to profit withal. For to one is given by the Spirit the word of wisdom; to another the word of knowledge by the same Spirit; to another faith by the same Spirit; to another the gifts of healing by the same Spirit; to another the working of miracles; to another prophecy; to another discerning of spirits; to another divers kinds of tongues; to another the interpretation of tongues: But all these worketh that one and the selfsame Spirit, dividing to every man severally as he will.   1 Corinthians 12:1, 4-11

Wherefore he saith, When he ascended up on high, he led captivity captive, and gave gifts unto men.   Ephesians 4:8

📖 Spiritual Maturity

But the path of the just is as the shining light, that shineth more and more unto the perfect day.   Proverbs 4:18

And he shall be like a tree planted by the rivers of water, that bringeth forth his fruit in his season; his leaf also shall not wither; and whatsoever he doeth shall prosper.   Psalm 1:3

The righteous shall flourish like the palm tree: he shall grow like a cedar in Lebanon. Those that be planted in the house of the LORD shall flourish in the courts of our God.

Psalm 92:12-13

Ye shall go forth, and grow up.   Malachi 4:2

And to know the love of Christ, which passeth knowledge, that ye might be filled with all the fullness of God.   Ephesians 3:19

That we henceforth be no more children, tossed to and fro, and carried about with every wind of doctrine...but speaking the truth in love, may grow up into him in all things, which is the head, even Christ.   Ephesians 4:14-15

Beside this, giving all diligence, add to your faith virtue; and to virtue knowledge...For if these things be in you, and abound, they make you that ye shall neither be barren nor unfruitful in the knowledge of our Lord Jesus Christ.   2 Peter 1:5, 8

Concerning...

But we all, with open face beholding as in a glass the glory of the Lord, are changed into the same image from glory to glory, even as by the Spirit of the Lord.　　2 Corinthians 3:18

Now therefore ye are...fellowcitizens with the saints, and of the household of God; and are built upon the foundation of the apostles and prophets, Jesus Christ himself being the chief corner stone; in whom all the building fitly framed together groweth unto an holy temple in the Lord: in whom ye also are builded together for an habitation of God through the Spirit.　　Ephesians 2:19-22

Being confident of this very thing, that he which hath begun a good work in you will perform it until the day of Jesus Christ.
Philippians 1:6

That ye might walk worthy of the Lord unto all pleasing, being fruitful in every good work, and increasing in the knowledge of God.
Colossians 1:10

As newborn babes, desire the sincere milk of the word, that ye may grow thereby: If so be ye have tasted that the Lord is gracious.
1 Peter 2:2-3

And this I pray, that your love may abound yet more and more in knowledge and in all judgment; That ye may approve things that are excellent; that ye may be sincere and without offense till the day of Christ; Being filled with the fruits of righteousness, which are by Jesus Christ, unto the glory and praise of God.   Philippians 1:9-11

Therefore leaving the principles of the doctrine of Christ, let us go on unto perfection.
                                        Hebrews 6:1

According as his divine power hath given unto us all things that pertain unto life and godliness, through the knowledge of him that hath called us to glory and virtue.   2 Peter 1:3

But grow in grace, and in the knowledge of our Lord and Savior Jesus Christ. To him be glory both now and for ever.   2 Peter 3:18

📖 STRENGTH

Blessed is the man whose strength is in thee; in whose heart are the ways of them...They go from strength to strength, every one of them in Zion appeareth before God.
                                        Psalm 84:5, 7

Concerning...

Glory and honor are in his presence; strength and gladness are in his place. 1 Chronicles 16:27

Both riches and honor come of thee, and thou reignest over all; and in thine hand is power and might; and in thine hand it is to make great, and to give strength unto all.
1 Chronicles 29:12

The LORD is my strength and my shield; my heart trusted in him, and I am helped: therefore my heart greatly rejoiceth; and with my song will I praise him. Psalm 28:7

The LORD will give strength unto his people.
Psalm 29:11

In the day when I cried thou answeredst me, and strengthenedst me with strength in my soul. Psalm 138:3

Trust ye in the LORD for ever: for in the LORD JEHOVAH is everlasting strength. Isaiah 26:4

They that wait upon the LORD shall renew their strength; they shall mount up with wings as eagles; they shall run, and not be weary; and they shall walk, and not faint.
Isaiah 40:31

It is God that girdeth me with strength, and maketh my way perfect. Psalm 18:32

The LORD is my light and my salvation; whom shall I fear? the LORD is the strength of my life; of whom shall I be afraid?
Psalm 27:1

But the salvation of the righteous is of the LORD: he is their strength in the time of trouble. Psalm 37:39

Thy God hath commanded thy strength: strengthen, O God, that which thou hast wrought for us. Psalm 68:28

My flesh and my heart faileth: but God is the strength of my heart, and my portion for ever.
Psalm 73:26

I will strengthen thee; yea, I will help thee; yea, I will uphold thee with the right hand of my righteousness. Isaiah 41:10

And he said unto me, My grace is sufficient for thee: for my strength is made perfect in weakness. Most gladly therefore will I rather glory in my infirmities, that the power of Christ may rest upon me. 2 Corinthians 12:9

Concerning...

The joy of the LORD is your strength.

Nehemiah 8:10

The way of the LORD is strength to the upright.

Proverbs 10:29

A wise man is strong; yea, a man of knowledge increaseth strength.

Proverbs 24:5

He giveth power to the faint; and to them that have no might he increaseth strength.

Isaiah 40:29

Be strong in the Lord, and in the power of his might.

Ephesians 6:10

I can do all things through Christ which strengtheneth me.

Philippians 4:13

We also...do not cease to pray for you...that ye might be filled with the knowledge of his will in all wisdom and spiritual understanding; That ye might walk worthy of the Lord unto all pleasing, being fruitful in every good work, and increasing in the knowledge of God; strengthened with all might, according to his glorious power, unto all patience and longsuffering with joyfulness.

Colossians 1:9-11

📖 SUCCESS

The LORD was with him, and…made all that he did to prosper in his hand.　　Genesis 39:3

The LORD, before whom I walk, will send his angel with thee, and prosper thy way.
　　Genesis 24:40

Thou shalt keep therefore his statutes, and his commandments, which I command thee this day, that it may go well with thee, and with thy children after thee, and that thou mayest prolong thy days upon the earth, which the LORD thy God giveth thee, for ever.
　　Deuteronomy 4:40

Hear therefore, O Israel, and observe to do it; that it may be well with thee, and that ye may increase mightily, as the LORD God of thy fathers hath promised thee, in the land that floweth with milk and honey.　　Deuteronomy 6:3

This book of the law shall not depart out of thy mouth; but thou shalt meditate therein day and night, that thou mayest observe to do according to all that is written therein: for then thou shalt make thy way prosperous, and then thou shalt have good success.　　Joshua 1:8

Concerning...

Then shalt thou prosper, if thou takest heed to fulfill the statutes and judgments which the LORD charged Moses with concerning Israel: be strong, and of good courage; dread not, nor be dismayed.   1 Chronicles 22:13

As long as he sought the LORD, God made him to prosper.   2 Chronicles 26:5

Thou hast dealt well with thy servant, O LORD, according unto thy word.   Psalm 119:65

I [wisdom] love them that love me; and those that seek me early shall find me. Riches and honor are with me; yea, durable riches and righteousness. My fruit is better than gold, yea, than fine gold; and my revenue than choice silver. I lead in the way of righteousness, in the midst of the paths of judgment: That I may cause those that love me to inherit substance; and I will fill their treasures.

Proverbs 8:17-21

📖 TRUTH

But thou, O Lord, art a God full of compassion, and gracious, longsuffering, and plenteous in mercy and truth.   Psalm 86:15

Lead me in thy truth, and teach me: for thou art the God of my salvation; on thee do I wait all the day…All the paths of the LORD are mercy and truth unto such as keep his covenant and his testimonies.　　　Psalm 25:5, 10

Behold, thou desirest truth in the inward parts: and in the hidden part thou shalt make me to know wisdom.　　　Psalm 51:6

Then said Jesus…If ye continue in my word, then are ye my disciples indeed; And ye shall know the truth, and the truth shall make you free.　　　John 8:31-32

But when the Comforter is come, whom I will send unto you from the Father, even the Spirit of truth, which proceedeth from the Father, he shall testify of me.　　　John 15:26

Howbeit when he, the Spirit of truth, is come, he will guide you into all truth: for he shall not speak of himself; but whatsoever he shall hear, that shall he speak: and he will show you things to come.　　　John 16:13

[God] Who will have all men to be saved, and to come unto the knowledge of the truth.
　　　1 Timothy 2:4

Concerning...

For the fruit of the Spirit is in all goodness and righteousness and truth.   Ephesians 5:9

For the truth's sake, which dwelleth in us, and shall be with us for ever. Grace be with you, mercy, and peace, from God the Father, and from the Lord Jesus Christ, the Son of the Father, in truth and love.   2 John 2-3

📖 WISDOM

For the LORD giveth wisdom: out of his mouth cometh knowledge and understanding. He layeth up sound wisdom for the righteous: he is a buckler to them that walk uprightly.
      Proverbs 2:6-7

For wisdom is better than rubies; and all the things that may be desired are not to be compared to it. I wisdom dwell with prudence, and find out knowledge of witty inventions.
      Proverbs 8:11-12

The fear of the LORD is the beginning of wisdom: and the knowledge of the holy is understanding.   Proverbs 9:10

For God giveth to a man that is good in his sight wisdom, and knowledge.   Ecclesiastes 2:26

Wisdom and knowledge is granted unto thee.
2 Chronicles 1:12

And unto man he said, Behold, the fear of the Lord, that is wisdom; and to depart from evil is understanding. Job 28:28

Behold, thou desirest truth in the inward parts: and in the hidden part thou shalt make me to know wisdom. Psalm 51:6

When wisdom entereth into thine heart, and knowledge is pleasant unto thy soul.
Proverbs 2:10

Blessed be the name of God for ever and ever: for wisdom and might are his...he giveth wisdom unto the wise, and knowledge to them that know understanding: He revealeth the deep and secret things.
Daniel 2:20-22

But of him are ye in Christ Jesus, who of God is made unto us wisdom. 1 Corinthians 1:30

If any of you lack wisdom, let him ask of God, that giveth to all men liberally, and upbraideth not; and it shall be given him.
James 1:5

Concerning...

📖 YOUR HEART'S DESIRES

Thou hast given him his heart's desire, and hast not withholden the request of his lips.

Psalm 21:2

Delight thyself also in the LORD; and he shall give thee the desires of thine heart.

Psalm 37:4

Who satisfieth thy mouth with good things; so that thy youth is renewed like the eagle's.

Psalm 103:5

Thou openest thine hand, and satisfiest the desire of every living thing. Psalm 145:16

I thank thee, and praise thee, O thou God of my fathers, who hast given me wisdom and might, and hast made known unto me now what we desired of thee. Daniel 2:23

The desire of the righteous shall be granted.

Proverbs 10:24

But now they desire a better country, that is, an heavenly: wherefore God is not ashamed to be called their God: for he hath prepared for them a city. Hebrews 11:16

And all Judah rejoiced at the oath: for they had sworn with all their heart, and sought him with their whole desire; and he was found of them: and the LORD gave them rest round about.   2 Chronicles 15:15

LORD, thou hast heard the desire of the humble: thou wilt prepare their heart, thou wilt cause thine ear to hear: to judge the fatherless and the oppressed, that the man of the earth may no more oppress.   Psalm 10:17–18

The God of my mercy shall prevent me: God shall let me see my desire.   Psalm 59:10

Whom have I in heaven but thee? and there is none upon earth that I desire beside thee. My flesh and my heart faileth: but God is the strength of my heart, and my portion for ever.
                    Psalm 73:25-26

A good man showeth favor, and lendeth: he will guide his affairs with discretion…His heart is established, he shall not be afraid, until he see his desire.   Psalm 112:5, 8

Hope deferred maketh the heart sick: but when the desire cometh, it is a tree of life.
                    Proverbs 13:12

Concerning...

He bringeth them unto their desired haven.

Psalm 107:30

He will fulfill the desire of them that fear him.

Psalm 145:19

What things soever ye desire, when ye pray, believe that ye receive them, and ye shall have them.

Mark 11:24

📖 Bible Promises For Those Who Are...

📖 AFRAID

The LORD is my light and my salvation; whom shall I fear? the LORD is the strength of my life; of whom shall I be afraid?   Psalm 27:1

What time I am afraid, I will trust in thee. In God I will praise his word, in God I have put my trust; I will not fear what flesh can do unto me.   Psalm 56:3-4

But now thus saith the LORD that created thee...Fear not: for I have redeemed thee, I have called thee by thy name; thou art mine.
                              Isaiah 43:1

He shall cover thee with his feathers, and under his wings shalt thou trust: his truth shall be thy shield and buckler. Thou shalt not be afraid for the terror by night; nor for the arrow that flieth by day; Nor for the pestilence that walketh in darkness; nor for the destruction that wasteth at noonday.   Psalm 91:4-6

Blessed is the man that feareth the LORD, that delighteth greatly in his commandments... He shall not be afraid of evil tidings: his heart is fixed, trusting in the LORD. His heart is established, he shall not be afraid.
Psalm 112:1, 7-8

Fear thou not; for I am with thee: be not dismayed; for I am thy God: I will strengthen thee; yea, I will help thee; yea, I will uphold thee with the right hand of my righteousness.
Isaiah 41:10

Say to them that are of a fearful heart, Be strong, fear not: behold, your God will come with vengeance, even God with a recompense; he will come and save you.   Isaiah 35:4

For I the LORD thy God will hold thy right hand, saying unto thee, Fear not; I will help thee.   Isaiah 41:13

For Those Who Are...

When thou goest out to battle against thine enemies, and seest horses, and chariots, and a people more than thou, be not afraid of them: for the LORD thy God is with thee, which brought thee up out of the land of Egypt.... Hear, O Israel, ye approach this day unto battle against your enemies: let not your hearts faint, fear not, and do not tremble, neither be ye terrified because of them; For the LORD your God is he that goeth with you, to fight for you against your enemies, to save you. *Deuteronomy 20:1, 3-4*

Fear not: for they that be with us are more than they that be with them. *2 Kings 6:16*

Be not afraid of sudden fear, neither of the desolation of the wicked, when it cometh. For the LORD shall be thy confidence, and shall keep thy foot from being taken.
Proverbs 3:25-26

Fear not, little flock; for it is your Father's good pleasure to give you the kingdom.
Luke 12:32

God hath not given us the spirit of fear; but of power, and of love, and of a sound mind.
2 Timothy 1:7

Be strong and of good courage, and do it: fear not, nor be dismayed: for the LORD God, even my God, will be with thee; he will not fail thee, nor forsake thee.   1 Chronicles 28:20

Are not five sparrows sold for two farthings, and not one of them is forgotten before God? But even the very hairs of your head are all numbered. Fear not therefore: ye are of more value than many sparrows.   Luke 12:6-7

There is no fear in love; but perfect love casteth out fear.   1 John 4:18

📖 BACKSLIDDEN

For thus saith the high and lofty One that inhabiteth eternity, whose name is Holy; I dwell in the high and holy place, with him also that is of a contrite and humble spirit, to revive the spirit of the humble, and to revive the heart of the contrite ones...I have seen his ways, and will heal him: I will lead him also, and restore comforts unto him and to his mourners. I create the fruit of the lips; Peace, peace to him that is far off, and to him that is near, saith the LORD; and I will heal him.
        Isaiah 57:15, 18-19

For Those Who Are...

I have blotted out, as a thick cloud, thy transgressions, and, as a cloud, thy sins: return unto
me; for I have redeemed thee.   Isaiah 44:22

Return, thou backsliding Israel, saith the
LORD; and I will not cause mine anger to fall
upon you: for I am merciful, saith the LORD,
and I will not keep anger for ever. Only acknowledge thine iniquity, that thou hast
transgressed against the LORD thy God, and
hast scattered thy ways to the strangers under
every green tree, and ye have not obeyed my
voice, saith the LORD. Turn, O backsliding
children, saith the LORD; for I am married
unto you: and I will take you one of a city,
and two of a family, and I will bring you to
Zion.   Jeremiah 3:12-14

O Israel, return unto the LORD thy God; for thou
hast fallen by thine iniquity. Take with you
words, and turn to the LORD: say unto him,
Take away all iniquity, and receive us gra-
ciously: so will we render the calves of our lips.
Asshur shall not save us; we will not ride upon
horses: neither will we say any more to the
work of our hands, Ye are our gods: for in thee
the fatherless findeth mercy. I will heal their
backsliding, I will love them freely: for mine
anger is turned away from him.   Hosea 14:1-4

Come now, and let us reason together, saith the LORD: though your sins be as scarlet, they shall be as white as snow; though they be red like crimson, they shall be as wool.

Isaiah 1:18

All we like sheep have gone astray; we have turned every one to his own way; and the LORD hath laid on him the iniquity of us all.

Isaiah 53:6

A voice was heard upon the high places, weeping and supplications of the children of Israel: for they have perverted their way, and they have forgotten the LORD their God. Return, ye backsliding children, and I will heal your backslidings. Behold, we come unto thee; for thou art the LORD our God.

Jeremiah 3:21-22

For I will set mine eyes upon them for good, and I will bring them again to this land: and I will build them, and not pull them down; and I will plant them, and not pluck them up. And I will give them an heart to know me, that I am the LORD: and they shall be my people, and I will be their God: for they shall return unto me with their whole heart.

Jeremiah 24:6-7

For Those Who Are...

📖 BROKENHEARTED

The LORD is nigh unto them that are of a broken heart; and saveth such as be of a contrite spirit.   Psalm 34:18

Thou tellest my wanderings: put thou my tears into thy bottle: are they not in thy book? When I cry unto thee, then shall mine enemies turn back: this I know; for God is for me.
                                     Psalm 56:8-9

He healeth the broken in heart, and bindeth up their wounds.   Psalm 147:3

Sing, O heavens; and be joyful, O earth; and break forth into singing, O mountains: for the LORD hath comforted his people, and will have mercy upon his afflicted.   Isaiah 49:13

The spirit of the Lord GOD is upon me; because the LORD hath anointed me to preach good tidings unto the meek; he hath sent me to bind up the brokenhearted...to comfort all that mourn.   Isaiah 61:1-2

He hath sent me to heal the brokenhearted, ...to set at liberty them that are bruised.
                                     Luke 4:18

Weeping may endure for a night, but joy cometh in the morning. Psalm 30:5

The sacrifices of God are a broken spirit: a broken and a contrite heart, O God, thou wilt not despise. Psalm 51:17

📖 BURDENED

Thou wilt surely wear away, both thou, and this people that is with thee: for this thing is too heavy for thee; thou art not able to perform it thyself alone...And it shall be, that every great matter they shall bring unto thee, but every small matter they shall judge: so shall it be easier for thyself, and they shall bear the burden with thee. Exodus 18:18, 22

And it shall come to pass in that day, that his burden shall be taken away from off thy shoulder, and his yoke from off thy neck, and the yoke shall be destroyed because of the anointing. Isaiah 10:27

Is not this the fast that I have chosen? to loose the bands of wickedness, to undo the heavy burdens, and to let the oppressed go free, and that ye break every yoke? Isaiah 58:6

For Those Who Are...

Blessed be the Lord, who daily loadeth us with benefits, even the God of our salvation.
Psalm 68:19

I removed his shoulder from the burden: his hands were delivered from the pots. Thou calledst in trouble, and I delivered thee; I answered thee in the secret place of thunder.
Psalm 81:6-7

[The LORD] which keepeth truth for ever... raiseth them that are bowed down: the LORD loveth the righteous.　　Psalm 146:6, 8

For thou hast broken the yoke of his burden, and the staff of his shoulder, the rod of his oppressor...For unto us a child is born, unto us a son is given: and the government shall be upon his shoulder: and his name shall be called Wonderful, Counselor, The mighty God, The everlasting Father, The Prince of Peace.　　Isaiah 9:4, 6

Come unto me, all ye that labor and are heavy laden, and I will give you rest. Take my yoke upon you, and learn of me; for I am meek and lowly in heart: and ye shall find rest unto your souls. For my yoke is easy, and my burden is light.　　Matthew 11:28-30

Cast thy burden upon the LORD, and he shall sustain thee: he shall never suffer the righteous to be moved .   Psalm 55:22

Casting all your care upon him; for he careth for you.   1 Peter 5:7

📖 CONFUSED

And thine ears shall hear a word behind thee, saying, This is the way, walk ye in it, when ye turn to the right hand, and when ye turn to the left.   Isaiah 30:21

But he that is spiritual judgeth all things... For who hath known the mind of the Lord, that he may instruct him? But we have the mind of Christ.   1 Corinthians 2:15-16

If any of you lack wisdom, let him ask of God, that giveth to all men liberally, and upbraideth not; and it shall be given him. But let him ask in faith, nothing wavering. For he that wavereth is like a wave of the sea driven with the wind and tossed. For let not that man think that he shall receive any thing of the Lord. A double minded man is unstable in all his ways.   James 1:5-8

They cried unto thee, and were delivered: they trusted in thee, and were not confounded.   Psalm 22:5

And I will bring the blind by a way that they knew not; I will lead them in paths that they have not known: I will make darkness light before them, and crooked things straight. These things will I do unto them, and not forsake them.   Isaiah 42:16

God is not the author of confusion, but of peace.   1 Corinthians 14:33

We are troubled on every side, yet not distressed; we are perplexed, but not in despair... that the life also of Jesus might be made manifest in our body. For we which live are alway delivered unto death for Jesus' sake, that the life also of Jesus might be made manifest in our mortal flesh.
                         2 Corinthians 4:8, 10-11

For where envying and strife is, there is confusion and every evil work. But the wisdom that is from above is first pure, then peaceable, gentle, and easy to be entreated, full of mercy and good fruits, without partiality, and without hypocrisy.   James 3:16-17

Thou wilt keep him in perfect peace, whose mind is stayed on thee.   Isaiah 26:3

For my thoughts are not your thoughts, neither are your ways my ways, saith the LORD. For as the heavens are higher than the earth, so are my ways higher than your ways, and my thoughts than your thoughts. Isaiah 55:8-9

📖 DEPRESSED

The LORD also will be a refuge for the oppressed, a refuge in times of trouble. They that know thy name will put their trust in thee: for thou, LORD, hast not forsaken them that seek thee.   Psalm 9:9-10

He brought me up also out of an horrible pit, out of the miry clay, and set my feet upon a rock, and established my goings.   Psalm 40:2

My flesh and my heart faileth: but God is the strength of my heart, and my portion for ever.
                    Psalm 73:26

My soul melteth for heaviness: strengthen thou me according unto thy word.
                    Psalm 119:28

For Those Who Are...

Neither be ye sorry; for the joy of the LORD is your strength....Hold your peace, for the day is holy; neither be ye grieved.   Nehemiah 8:10-11

Be of good courage, and he shall strengthen your heart, all ye that hope in the LORD.
                                        Psalm 31:24

Why art thou cast down, O my soul? and why art thou disquieted within me? hope in God: for I shall yet praise him, who is the health of my countenance, and my God.   Psalm 43:5

Heaviness in the heart of man maketh it stoop: but a good word maketh it glad.
                                        Proverbs 12:25

To appoint unto them that mourn in Zion, to give unto them beauty for ashes, the oil of joy for mourning, the garment of praise for the spirit of heaviness; that they might be called trees of righteousness, the planting of the LORD, that he might be glorified.   Isaiah 61:3

Then shall the virgin rejoice in the dance, both young men and old together: for I will turn their mourning into joy, and will comfort them, and make them rejoice from their sorrow.   Jeremiah 31:13

Thou hast turned for me my mourning into dancing: thou hast put off my sackcloth, and girded me with gladness. Psalm 30:11

And the ransomed of the LORD shall return, and come to Zion with songs and everlasting joy upon their heads: they shall obtain joy and gladness, and sorrow and sighing shall flee away. Isaiah 35:10

Wherein ye greatly rejoice, though now for a season, if need be, ye are in heaviness through manifold temptations....Whom having not seen, ye love; in whom, though now ye see him not, yet believing, ye rejoice with joy unspeakable and full of glory. 1 Peter 1:6, 8

📖 DISCOURAGED

A bruised reed shall he not break, and the smoking flax shall he not quench: he shall bring forth judgment unto truth. He shall not fail nor be discouraged, till he have set judgment in the earth: and the isles shall wait for his law. Isaiah 42:3-4

Let us not be weary in well doing: for in due season we shall reap, if we faint not.

Galatians 6:9

For Those Who Are...

But verily God hath heard me; he hath attended to the voice of my prayer. Blessed be God, which hath not turned away my prayer, nor his mercy from me.   Psalm 66:19-20

For thus saith the Lord GOD, the Holy One of Israel; In returning and rest shall ye be saved; in quietness and in confidence shall be your strength.   Isaiah 30:15

Hope maketh not ashamed; because the love of God is shed abroad in our hearts by the Holy Ghost which is given unto us. Romans 5:5

We know that all things work together for good to them that love God, to them who are the called according to his purpose.
                    Romans 8:28

Being confident of this very thing, that he which hath begun a good work in you will perform it until the day of Jesus Christ.
                    Philippians 1:6

Cast not away therefore your confidence, which hath great recompense of reward. For ye have need of patience, that, after ye have done the will of God, ye might receive the promise.   Hebrews 10:35-36

I had fainted, unless I had believed to see the goodness of the LORD in the land of the living. Wait on the LORD: be of good courage, and he shall strengthen thine heart: wait, I say, on the LORD.   Psalm 27:13-14

Our soul waiteth for the LORD: he is our help and our shield. For our heart shall rejoice in him, because we have trusted in his holy name. Let thy mercy, O LORD, be upon us, according as we hope in thee.   Psalm 33:20-22

Trust in him at all times; ye people, pour out your heart before him: God is a refuge for us.
                                          Psalm 62:8

📖 DOUBTING

Jesus answering saith unto them, Have faith in God. For verily I say unto you, That whosoever shall say unto this mountain, Be thou removed, and be thou cast into the sea; and shall not doubt in his heart, but shall believe that those things which he saith shall come to pass; he shall have whatsoever he saith. Therefore I say unto you, What things soever ye desire, when ye pray, believe that ye receive them, and ye shall have them.   Mark 11:22-24

For Those Who Are...

Hast thou faith? have it to thyself before God. Happy is he that condemneth not himself in that thing which he alloweth. And he that doubteth is damned if he eat, because he eateth not of faith: for whatsoever is not of faith is sin. Romans 14:22-23

Beloved, if our heart condemn us not, then have we confidence toward God. And whatsoever we ask, we receive of him, because we keep his commandments, and do those things that are pleasing in his sight. 1 John 3:21-22

If we believe not, yet he abideth faithful: he cannot deny himself. 2 Timothy 2:13

Let us draw near with a true heart in full assurance of faith, having our hearts sprinkled from an evil conscience, and our bodies washed with pure water. Let us hold fast the profession of our faith without wavering, for he is faithful that promised. Hebrews 10:22-23

Now faith is the substance of things hoped for, the evidence of things not seen....But without faith it is impossible to please him: for he that cometh to God must believe that he is, and that he is a rewarder of them that diligently seek him. Hebrews 11:1, 6

Jesus said unto him, If thou canst believe, all things are possible to him that believeth. And straightway the father of the child cried out, and said with tears, Lord, I believe; help thou mine unbelief. Mark 9:23-24

I will therefore that men pray every where, lifting up holy hands, without wrath and doubting. 1 Timothy 2:8

📖 Facing Death

Yea, though I walk through the valley of the shadow of death, I will fear no evil: for thou art with me; thy rod and thy staff they comfort me. Psalm 23:4

O death, where is thy sting? O grave, where is thy victory? The sting of death is sin; and the strength of sin is the law. But thanks be to God, which giveth us the victory through our Lord Jesus Christ. 1 Corinthians 15:55-57

We are confident, I say, and willing rather to be absent from the body, and to be present with the Lord. Wherefore we labor, that, whether present or absent, we may be accepted of him. 2 Corinthians 5:8-9

For Those Who Are...

In my Father's house are many mansions: if it were not so, I would have told you. I go to prepare a place for you. And if I go and prepare a place for you, I will come again, and receive you unto myself; that where I am, there ye may be also.   John 14:2-3

For I am persuaded, that neither death, nor life, nor angels, nor principalities, nor powers, nor things present, nor things to come, Nor height, nor depth, nor any other creature, shall be able to separate us from the love of God, which is in Christ Jesus our Lord.
Romans 8:38-39

For this corruptible must put on incorruption, and this mortal must put on immortality. So when this corruptible shall have put on incorruption, and this mortal shall have put on immortality, then shall be brought to pass the saying that is written, Death is swallowed up in victory.   1 Corinthians 15:53-54

I would not have you to be ignorant, brethren, concerning them which are asleep, that ye sorrow not, even as others which have no hope. For if we believe that Jesus died and rose again, even so them also which sleep in Jesus will God bring with him.   1 Thessalonians 4:13-14

Jesus said unto her, I am the resurrection, and the life: he that believeth in me, though he were dead, yet shall he live.   John 11:25

📖 FAITHFUL

O love the LORD, all ye his saints: for the LORD preserveth the faithful.   Psalm 31:23

Mine eyes shall be upon the faithful of the land, that they may dwell with me: he that walketh in a perfect way, he shall serve me.
                                    Psalm 101:6

A faithful man shall abound with blessings: but he that maketh haste to be rich shall not be innocent.   Proverbs 28:20

He that is faithful in that which is least is faithful also in much: and he that is unjust in the least is unjust also in much.   Luke 16:10

Fear none of those things which thou shalt suffer: behold, the devil shall cast some of you into prison, that ye may be tried; and ye shall have tribulation ten days: be thou faithful unto death, and I will give thee a crown of life.   Revelation 2:10

For Those Who Are...

Let not mercy and truth forsake thee: bind them about thy neck; write them upon the table of thine heart: so shalt thou find favor and good understanding in the sight of God and man.   Proverbs 3:3-4

Most men will proclaim every one his own goodness: but a faithful man who can find? The just man walketh in his integrity: his children are blessed after him.   Proverbs 20:6-7

As the cold of snow in the time of harvest, so is a faithful messenger to them that send him: for he refresheth the soul of his masters.
                                                     Proverbs 25:13

📖 FORSAKEN

For the LORD God, even my God, will be with thee; he will not fail thee, nor forsake thee.
                                        1 Chronicles 28:20

Thou shalt no more be termed Forsaken; neither shall thy land any more be termed Desolate: but thou shalt be called Hephzibah, and thy land Beulah: for the LORD delighteth in thee, and thy land shall be married.
                                               Isaiah 62:4

For the LORD thy God is a merciful God; he will not forsake thee, neither destroy thee, nor forget the covenant of thy fathers which he sware unto them.   Deuteronomy 4:31

For the LORD will not forsake his people for his great name's sake: because it hath pleased the LORD to make you his people.
          1 Samuel 12:22

They that know thy name will put their trust in thee: for thou, LORD, hast not forsaken them that seek thee.   Psalm 9:10

I have been young, and now am old; yet have I not seen the righteous forsaken…For the LORD loveth judgment, and forsaketh not his saints.   Psalm 37:25, 28

Can a woman forget her sucking child, that she should not have compassion on the son of her womb? yea, they may forget, yet will I not forget thee.   Isaiah 49:15

For the LORD hath called thee as a woman forsaken and grieved in spirit, and a wife of youth, when thou wast refused, saith thy God…with great mercies will I gather thee.
          Isaiah 54:6-7

For the LORD will not cast off his people, neither will he forsake his inheritance.   Psalm 94:14

There is a friend that sticketh closer than a brother.   Proverbs 18:24

He hath said, I will never leave thee, nor forsake thee.   Hebrews 13:5

📖 GODLY

But know that the LORD hath set apart him that is godly for himself: the LORD will hear when I call unto him.   Psalm 4:3

The LORD knoweth the days of the upright: their inheritance shall be forever. They shall not be ashamed in the evil time: in the days of famine they shall be satisfied.   Psalm 37:18-19

Add to your faith virtue; and to virtue knowledge; and to knowledge temperance; and to temperance patience; and to patience godliness; and to godliness brotherly kindness; and to brotherly kindness charity. For if these things be in you, and abound, they make you that ye shall neither be barren nor unfruitful in the knowledge of our Lord Jesus Christ.   2 Peter 1:5-8

My defense is of God, which saveth the upright in heart. Psalm 7:10

O continue thy lovingkindness unto them that know thee; and thy righteousness to the upright in heart. Psalm 36:10

The steps of a good man are ordered by the LORD: and he delighteth in his way. Though he fall, he shall not be utterly cast down: for the LORD upholdeth him with his hand.
Psalm 37:23-24

Light is sown for the righteous, and gladness for the upright in heart. Psalm 97:11

When a man's ways please the LORD, he maketh even his enemies to be at peace with him. Proverbs 16:7

But godliness with contentment is great gain.
1 Timothy 6:6

Godliness is profitable unto all things, having promise of the life that now is, and of that which is to come. 1 Timothy 4:8

The Lord knoweth how to deliver the godly out of temptations. 2 Peter 2:9

For Those Who Are...

📖 GUILTY

Blessed is he whose transgression is forgiven, whose sin is covered. Blessed is the man unto whom the LORD imputeth not iniquity, and in whose spirit there is no guile.   Psalm 32:1-2

I, even I, am he that blotteth out thy transgressions for mine own sake, and will not remember thy sins.   Isaiah 43:25

For God sent not his Son into the world to condemn the world; but that the world through him might be saved. He that believeth on him is not condemned: but he that believeth not is condemned already, because he hath not believed in the name of the only begotten Son of God.   John 3:17-18

Be it known unto you therefore, men and brethren, that through this man is preached unto you the forgiveness of sins: And by him all that believe are justified from all things, from which ye could not be justified by the law of Moses.   Acts 13:38-39

For I will be merciful to their unrighteousness, and their sins and their iniquities will I remember no more.   Hebrews 8:12

He hath not dealt with us after our sins; nor rewarded us according to our iniquities. For as the heaven is high above the earth, so great is his mercy toward them that fear him. As far as the east is from the west, so far hath he removed our transgressions from us.

Psalm 103:10-12

Let the wicked forsake his way, and the unrighteous man his thoughts: and let him return unto the LORD, and he will have mercy upon him; and to our God, for he will abundantly pardon.

Isaiah 55:7

There is therefore now no condemnation to them which are in Christ Jesus, who walk not after the flesh, but after the Spirit. For the law of the Spirit of life in Christ Jesus hath made me free from the law of sin and death.

Romans 8:1-2

How much more shall the blood of Christ, who through the eternal Spirit offered himself without spot to God, purge your conscience from dead works to serve the living God?

Hebrews 9:14

For if our heart condemn us, God is greater than our heart, and knoweth all things.   1 John 3:20

If we confess our sins, he is faithful and just to forgive us our sins, and to cleanse us from all unrighteousness.   1 John 1:9

📖 HELPLESS

He shall deliver thee in six troubles: yea, in seven there shall no evil touch thee.   Job 5:19

The LORD also will be a refuge for the oppressed, a refuge in times of trouble.   Psalm 9:9

The poor committeth himself unto thee; thou art the helper of the fatherless.   Psalm 10:14

For I the LORD thy God will hold thy right hand, saying unto thee, Fear not; I will help thee.   Isaiah 41:13

Likewise the Spirit also helpeth our infirmities: for we know not what we should pray for as we ought: but the Spirit itself maketh intercession for us with groanings which cannot be uttered.   Romans 8:26

And he said unto me, My grace is sufficient for thee: for my strength is made perfect in weakness.   2 Corinthians 12:9

God is mine helper: the Lord is with them that uphold my soul.   Psalm 54:4

I can do all things through Christ which strengtheneth me.   Philippians 4:13

Let us therefore come boldly unto the throne of grace, that we may obtain mercy, and find grace to help in time of need.   Hebrews 4:16

So that we may boldly say, The Lord is my helper, and I will not fear what man shall do unto me.   Hebrews 13:6

Greater is he that is in you, than he that is in the world.   1 John 4:4

📖 HONEST

LORD, who shall abide in thy tabernacle? who shall dwell in thy holy hill? He that walketh uprightly, and worketh righteousness, and speaketh the truth in his heart.   Psalm 15:1-2

Keep thy heart with all diligence; for out of it are the issues of life. Put away from thee a froward mouth, and perverse lips put far from thee.   Proverbs 4:23-24

For Those Who Are...

Who shall ascend into the hill of the LORD? or who shall stand in his holy place? He that hath clean hands, and a pure heart; who hath not lifted up his soul unto vanity, nor sworn deceitfully. He shall receive the blessing from the LORD, and righteousness from the God of his salvation.　　　　　　　　Psalm 24:3-5

What man is he that desireth life, and loveth many days, that he may see good? Keep thy tongue from evil, and thy lips from speaking guile.　　　　　　　　Psalm 34:12-13

The wicked is snared by the transgression of his lips: but the just shall come out of trouble.
　　　　　　　　Proverbs 12:13

Lying lips are abomination to the LORD: but they that deal truly are his delight.
　　　　　　　　Proverbs 12:22

He that walketh righteously, and speaketh uprightly; he that despiseth the gain of oppressions, that shaketh his hands from holding of bribes...He shall dwell on high...bread shall be given him; his waters shall be sure. Thine eyes shall see the king in his beauty: they shall behold the land that is very far off.
　　　　　　　　Isaiah 33:15-17

A man shall be satisfied with good by the fruit of his mouth. Proverbs 12:14

The lip of truth shall be established for ever: but a lying tongue is but for a moment.
Proverbs 12:19

📖 IMPATIENT

Wait on the LORD: be of good courage, and he shall strengthen thine heart: wait, I say, on the LORD. Psalm 27:14

Rest in the LORD, and wait patiently for him: fret not thyself because of him who prospereth in his way. Psalm 37:7

Wait on the LORD, and keep his way, and he shall exalt thee to inherit the land.
Psalm 37:34

And not only so, but we glory in tribulations also: knowing that tribulation worketh patience; And patience, experience; and experience, hope: And hope maketh not ashamed; because the love of God is shed abroad in our hearts by the Holy Ghost which is given unto us. Romans 5:3–5

That ye be not slothful, but followers of them who through faith and patience inherit the promises.   Hebrews 6:12

Cast not away therefore your confidence, which hath great recompense of reward. For ye have need of patience, that, after ye have done the will of God, ye might receive the promise.   Hebrews 10:35-36

Knowing this, that the trying of your faith worketh patience. But let patience have her perfect work, that ye may be perfect and entire, wanting nothing.   James 1:3-4

📖 LONELY

God setteth the solitary in families: he bringeth out those which are bound with chains.   Psalm 68:6

When thou passest through the waters, I will be with thee; and through the rivers, they shall not overflow thee: when thou walkest through the fire, thou shalt not be burned; neither shall the flame kindle upon thee...Fear not: for I am with thee.
                    Isaiah 43:2, 5

When my father and my mother forsake me, then the LORD will take me up.   Psalm 27:10

I the LORD have called thee in righteousness, and will hold thine hand, and will keep thee.
Isaiah 42:6

For the mountains shall depart, and the hills be removed; but my kindness shall not depart from thee, neither shall the covenant of my peace be removed, saith the LORD that hath mercy on thee.   Isaiah 54:10

Lo, I am with you alway, even unto the end of the world.   Matthew 28:20

I will not leave you comfortless: I will come to you.   John 14:18

For he hath said, I will never leave thee, nor forsake thee.   Hebrews 13:5

📖 PERSECUTED

And ye shall be hated of all men for my name's sake. But there shall not an hair of your head perish. In your patience possess ye your souls.   Luke 21:17-19

For Those Who Are...

Blessed are they which are persecuted for righteousness' sake: for theirs is the kingdom of heaven.

Matthew 5:10

Blessed are ye, when men shall revile you, and persecute you, and shall say all manner of evil against you falsely, for my sake. Rejoice, and be exceeding glad: for great is your reward in heaven: for so persecuted they the prophets which were before you.

Matthew 5:11-12

Love your enemies, bless them that curse you, do good to them that hate you, and pray for them which despitefully use you, and persecute you; That ye may be the children of your Father which is in heaven.

Matthew 5:44-45

But before all these, they shall lay their hands on you, and persecute you, delivering you up to the synagogues, and into prisons, being brought before kings and rulers for my name's sake. And it shall turn to you for a testimony. Settle it therefore in your hearts, not to meditate before what ye shall answer: For I will give you a mouth and wisdom, which all your adversaries shall not be able to gainsay nor resist.

Luke 21:12-15

We are troubled on every side, yet not distressed; we are perplexed, but not in despair; Persecuted, but not forsaken; cast down, but not destroyed.   2 Corinthians 4:8-9

It is a faithful saying: For if we be dead with him, we shall also live with him: If we suffer, we shall also reign with him.
                                        2 Timothy 2:11-12

📖 PERSONALLY ATTACKED

Fear ye not, stand still, and see the salvation of the LORD, which he will show to you to day...The LORD shall fight for you, and ye shall hold your peace.   Exodus 14:13-14

But the salvation of the righteous is of the LORD: he is their strength in the time of trouble. And the LORD shall help them, and deliver them: he shall deliver them from the wicked, and save them, because they trust in him.   Psalm 37:39-40

And they shall fight against thee, but they shall not prevail against thee: for I am with thee to save thee and to deliver thee, saith the LORD.   Jeremiah 15:20

For Those Who Are...

But let all those that put their trust in thee rejoice: let them ever shout for joy, because thou defendest them. Psalm 5:11

The LORD is my light and my salvation; whom shall I fear? the LORD is the strength of my life; of whom shall I be afraid? When the wicked, even mine enemies and my foes, came upon me to eat up my flesh, they stumbled and fell. Psalm 27:1-2

And I will deliver thee out of the hand of the wicked, and I will redeem thee out of the hand of the terrible. Jeremiah 15:21

Dearly beloved, avenge not yourselves, but rather give place unto wrath: for it is written, Vengeance is mine; I will repay, saith the Lord. Therefore if thine enemy hunger, feed him; if he thirst, give him drink: for in so doing thou shalt heap coals of fire on his head. Be not overcome of evil, but overcome evil with good. Romans 12:19-21

Not rendering evil for evil, or railing for railing: but contrariwise blessing; knowing that ye are thereunto called, that ye should inherit a blessing. 1 Peter 3:9

What shall we then say to these things? If God be for us, who can be against us?

Romans 8:31

📖 RIGHTEOUS

The righteous also shall hold on his way, and he that hath clean hands shall be stronger and stronger. Job 17:9

He withdraweth not his eyes from the righteous: but with kings are they on the throne; yea, he doth establish them for ever, and they are exalted. Job 36:7

The eyes of the LORD are upon the righteous, and his ears are open unto their cry. Psalm 34:15

The righteous cry, and the LORD heareth, and delivereth them out of all their troubles...Many are the afflictions of the righteous: but the LORD delivereth him out of them all. Psalm 34:17, 19

The LORD loveth the righteous. Psalm 146:8

He layeth up sound wisdom for the righteous: he is a buckler to them that walk uprightly. He keepeth the paths of judgment, and preserveth the way of his saints. Proverbs 2:7-8

For Those Who Are...

For thou, LORD, wilt bless the righteous; with favor wilt thou compass him as with a shield.
Psalm 5:12

God is in the generation of the righteous.
Psalm 14:5

I have been young, and now am old; yet have I not seen the righteous forsaken, nor his seed begging bread....The righteous shall inherit the land, and dwell therein forever.   Psalm 37:25, 29

The desire of the righteous shall be granted.
Proverbs 10:24

The hope of the righteous shall be gladness.... The way of the LORD is strength to the upright.
Proverbs 10:28-29

The righteous is an everlasting foundation.... The righteous shall never be removed.
Proverbs 10:25, 30

Then shall the righteous shine forth as the sun in the kingdom of their Father.   Matthew 13:43

They which receive abundance of grace and of the gift of righteousness shall reign in life by one, Jesus Christ.
Romans 5:17

📖 SICK

I will take sickness away from the midst of thee.   Exodus 23:25

And the LORD will take away from thee all sickness, and will put none of the evil diseases of Egypt, which thou knowest, upon thee.   Deuteronomy 7:15

Blessed is he that considereth the poor: the LORD will deliver him in time of trouble…The LORD will strengthen him upon the bed of languishing: thou wilt make all his bed in his sickness.   Psalm 41:1, 3

And these signs shall follow them that believe; In my name shall they cast out devils; they shall speak with new tongues…they shall lay hands on the sick, and they shall recover.   Mark 16:17-18

Is any sick among you? let him call for the elders of the church; and let them pray over him, anointing him with oil in the name of the Lord: And the prayer of faith shall save the sick, and the Lord shall raise him up; and if he have committed sins, they shall be forgiven him.   James 5:14-15

He cast out the spirits with his word, and healed all that were sick: That it might be fulfilled which was spoken by Esaias the prophet, saying, Himself took our infirmities, and bare our sicknesses.   Matthew 8:16-17

As many as touched [the hem of his garment] were made perfectly whole.   Matthew 14:36

📖 SORROWFUL

They that sow in tears shall reap in joy. He that goeth forth and weepeth, bearing precious seed, shall doubtless come again with rejoicing, bringing his sheaves with him.   Psalm 126:5-6

Then shall the virgin rejoice in the dance, both young men and old together: for I will turn their mourning into joy, and will comfort them, and make them rejoice from their sorrow.   Jeremiah 31:13

Blessed are they that mourn: for they shall be comforted.   Matthew 5:4

Ye now therefore have sorrow: but I will see you again, and your heart shall rejoice, and your joy no man taketh from you.   John 16:22

Weeping may endure for a night, but joy cometh in the morning.   Psalm 30:5

Sing, O heavens; and be joyful, O earth; and break forth into singing, O mountains: for the LORD hath comforted his people, and will have mercy upon his afflicted.   Isaiah 49:13

Therefore the redeemed of the LORD shall return, and come with singing unto Zion; and everlasting joy shall be upon their head: they shall obtain gladness and joy; and sorrow and mourning shall flee away.   Isaiah 51:11

And God shall wipe away all tears from their eyes; and there shall be no more death, neither sorrow, nor crying, neither shall there be any more pain: for the former things are passed away.   Revelation 21:4

📖 TEMPTED

Abstain from all appearance of evil. And the very God of peace sanctify you wholly; I pray God your whole spirit and soul and body be preserved blameless unto the coming of our Lord Jesus Christ. Faithful is he that calleth you, who also will do it. 1 Thessalonians 5:22-24

For Those Who Are...

There hath no temptation taken you but such as is common to man: but God is faithful, who will not suffer you to be tempted above that ye are able; but will with the temptation also make a way to escape, that ye may be able to bear it. — 1 Corinthians 10:13

For in that he himself hath suffered being tempted, he is able to succor them that are tempted. — Hebrews 2:18

Seeing then that we have a great high priest, that is passed into the heavens, Jesus the Son of God, let us hold fast our profession. For we have not an high priest which cannot be touched with the feeling of our infirmities; but was in all points tempted like as we are, yet without sin. Let us therefore come boldly unto the throne of grace, that we may obtain mercy, and find grace to help in time of need. — Hebrews 4:14-16

And delivered just Lot, vexed with the filthy conversation of the wicked: (For that righteous man dwelling among them, in seeing and hearing, vexed his righteous soul from day to day with their unlawful deeds;) The Lord knoweth how to deliver the godly out of temptations. — 2 Peter 2:7-9

Blessed is the man that endureth temptation: for when he is tried, he shall receive the crown of life, which the Lord hath promised to them that love him.   James 1:12

📖 UNDER SATANIC ATTACK

I pray not that thou shouldest take them out of the world, but that thou shouldest keep them from the evil. They are not of the world, even as I am not of the world.   John 17:15-16

Grace be to you and peace from God the Father, and from our Lord Jesus Christ, Who gave himself for our sins, that he might deliver us from this present evil world, according to the will of God and our Father.   Galatians 1:3-4

We know that whosoever is born of God sinneth not; but he that is begotten of God keepeth himself, and that wicked one toucheth him not.   1 John 5:18

Fear none of those things which thou shalt suffer: behold, the devil shall cast some of you into prison...be thou faithful unto death, and I will give thee a crown of life.
                              Revelation 2:10

And the God of peace shall bruise Satan under your feet shortly. The grace of our Lord Jesus Christ be with you.   Romans 16:20

Submit yourselves therefore to God. Resist the devil, and he will flee from you.   James 4:7

📖 WORRIED

In the multitude of my thoughts within me thy comforts delight my soul.   Psalm 94:19

Therefore take no thought, saying, What shall we eat? or, What shall we drink? or, Wherewithal shall we be clothed? (For after all these things do the Gentiles seek:) for your heavenly Father knoweth that ye have need of all these things. But seek ye first the kingdom of God, and his righteousness; and all these things shall be added unto you.
                              Matthew 6:31-33

Be careful for nothing; but in every thing by prayer and supplication with thanksgiving let your requests be made known unto God. And the peace of God, which passeth all understanding, shall keep your hearts and minds through Christ Jesus.   Philippians 4:6-7

Hear me when I call, O God of my righteousness: thou hast enlarged me when I was in distress; have mercy upon me, and hear my prayer. Psalm 4:1

Fret not thyself because of evildoers, neither be thou envious against the workers of iniquity. For they shall soon be cut down like the grass, and wither as the green herb. Trust in the LORD, and do good; so shalt thou dwell in the land, and verily thou shalt be fed. Delight thyself also in the LORD; and he shall give thee the desires of thine heart. Commit thy way unto the LORD; trust also in him; and he shall bring it to pass...Rest in the LORD, and wait patiently for him: fret not thyself because of him who prospereth in his way, because of the man who bringeth wicked devices to pass. Psalm 37:1-5, 7

Better is an handful with quietness, than both the hands full with travail and vexation of spirit. Ecclesiastes 4:6

Not that I speak in respect of want: for I have learned, in whatsoever state I am, therewith to be content...I can do all things through Christ which strengtheneth me.
Philippians 4:11, 13

For Those Who Are...

In my distress I called upon the LORD, and cried unto my God: he heard my voice out of his temple, and my cry came before him, even into his ears. Psalm 18:6

Though I walk in the midst of trouble, thou wilt revive me: thou shalt stretch forth thine hand against the wrath of mine enemies, and thy right hand shall save me. The LORD will perfect that which concerneth me: thy mercy, O LORD, endureth for ever: forsake not the works of thine own hands. Psalm 138:7-8

When your fear cometh as desolation, and your destruction cometh as a whirlwind; when distress and anguish cometh upon you...But whoso hearkeneth unto me shall dwell safely, and shall be quiet from fear of evil. Proverbs 1:27, 33

And which of you with taking thought can add to his stature one cubit? If ye then be not able to do that thing which is least, why take ye thought for the rest? Luke 12:25-26

Humble yourselves therefore under the mighty hand of God, that he may exalt you in due time: casting all your care upon him; for he careth for you. 1 Peter 5:6-7

Therefore I say unto you, Take no thought for your life, what ye shall eat, or what ye shall drink; nor yet for your body, what ye shall put on. Is not the life more than meat, and the body than raiment?…Therefore take no thought, saying, What shall we eat? or, What shall we drink? or, Wherewithal shall we be clothed? (For after all these things do the Gentiles seek:) for your heavenly Father knoweth that ye have need of all these things. But seek ye first the kingdom of God, and his righteousness; and all these things shall be added unto you. Take therefore no thought for the morrow: for the morrow shall take thought for the things of itself.

Matthew 6:25, 31–34

📖 Bible Promises For Those Who...

📖 Believe in Jesus Christ

He that believeth on me, as the scripture hath said, out of his belly shall flow rivers of living water.   John 7:38

Whosoever believeth that Jesus is the Christ is born of God: and every one that loveth him that begat loveth him also that is begotten of him.   1 John 5:1

Who is he that overcometh the world, but he that believeth that Jesus is the Son of God?
                                                  1 John 5:5

Verily, verily, I say unto you, He that heareth my word, and believeth on him that sent me, hath everlasting life, and shall not come into condemnation; but is passed from death unto life.   John 5:24

And Jesus said unto them, I am the bread of life: he that cometh to me shall never hunger; and he that believeth on me shall never thirst. …And this is the will of him that sent me, that every one which seeth the Son, and believeth on him, may have everlasting life: and I will raise him up at the last day.   John 6:35, 40

I am come a light into the world, that whosoever believeth on me should not abide in darkness.   John 12:46

Verily, verily, I say unto you, He that believeth on me, the works that I do shall he do also; and greater works than these shall he do; because I go unto my Father.   John 14:12

To him give all the prophets witness, that through his name whosoever believeth in him shall receive remission of sins.   Acts 10:43

For we which have believed do enter into rest.   Hebrews 4:3

For Those Who...

Jesus said unto him, If thou canst believe, all things are possible to him that believeth.

Mark 9:23

And whosoever liveth and believeth in me shall never die.

John 11:26

But to him that worketh not, but believeth on him that justifieth the ungodly, his faith is counted for righteousness.

Romans 4:5

Whosoever believeth on him shall not be ashamed.

Romans 9:33

📖 Do Good Deeds

Blessed is he that considereth the poor: the LORD will deliver him in time of trouble.

Psalm 41:1

He that hath pity upon the poor lendeth unto the LORD; and that which he hath given will he pay him again.

Proverbs 19:17

Whosoever shall give to drink unto one of these little ones a cup of cold water only in the name of a disciple, verily I say unto you, he shall in no wise lose his reward.

Matthew 10:42

Is [not a righteous fast] to deal thy bread to the hungry, and that thou bring the poor that are cast out to thy house? when thou seest the naked, that thou cover him; and that thou hide not thyself from thine own flesh? Then shall thy light break forth as the morning, and thine health shall spring forth speedily: and thy righteousness shall go before thee; the glory of the LORD shall be thy reward. Then shalt thou call, and the LORD shall answer; thou shalt cry, and he shall say, Here I am. If thou take away from the midst of thee the yoke, the putting forth of the finger, and speaking vanity; And if thou draw out thy soul to the hungry, and satisfy the afflicted soul; then shall thy light rise in obscurity, and thy darkness be as the noon day: And the LORD shall guide thee continually, and satisfy thy soul in drought, and make fat thy bones: and thou shalt be like a watered garden, and like a spring of water, whose waters fail not.   Isaiah 58:7-11

Let us not be weary in well doing: for in due season we shall reap, if we faint not.
Galatians 6:9

Let your light so shine before men, that they may see your good works, and glorify your Father which is in heaven.   Matthew 5:16

For Those Who...

Thou shalt surely give him [someone in need], and thine heart shall not be grieved when thou givest unto him: because that for this thing the LORD thy God shall bless thee in all thy works, and in all that thou puttest thine hand unto. For the poor shall never cease out of the land: therefore I command thee, saying, Thou shalt open thine hand wide unto thy brother, to thy poor, and to thy needy, in thy land. Deuteronomy 15:10-11

Who can find a virtuous woman? for her price is far above rubies....She stretcheth out her hand to the poor; yea, she reacheth forth her hands to the needy....Strength and honor are her clothing; and she shall rejoice in time to come....Her children arise up, and call her blessed; her husband also, and he praiseth her. Proverbs 31:10, 20, 25, 28

Charge them that are rich in this world, that they be not high-minded, nor trust in uncertain riches, but in the living God, who giveth us richly all things to enjoy; That they do good, that they be rich in good works, ready to distribute, willing to communicate; Laying up in store for themselves a good foundation against the time to come, that they may lay hold on eternal life. 1 Timothy 6:17-19

For I was an hungered, and ye gave me meat: I was thirsty, and ye gave me drink: I was a stranger, and ye took me in: Naked, and ye clothed me: I was sick, and ye visited me: I was in prison, and ye came unto me. Then shall the righteous answer him, saying, Lord, when saw we thee an hungered, and fed thee? or thirsty, and gave thee drink? When saw we thee a stranger, and took thee in? or naked, and clothed thee? Or when saw we thee sick, or in prison, and came unto thee? And the King shall answer and say unto them, Verily I say unto you, Inasmuch as ye have done it unto one of the least of these my brethren, ye have done it unto me.   Matthew 25:35-40

And the people asked him, saying, What shall we do then? He answereth and saith unto them, He that hath two coats, let him impart to him that hath none; and he that hath meat, let him do likewise.   Luke 3:10-11

For we are his workmanship, created in Christ Jesus unto good works, which God hath before ordained that we should walk in them.   Ephesians 2:10

For God is not unrighteous to forget your work and labor of love, which ye have showed

toward his name, in that ye have ministered to
the saints, and do minister. Hebrews 6:10

Hereby perceive we the love of God, because
he laid down his life for us: and we ought to
lay down our lives for the brethren. But
whoso hath this world's good, and seeth his
brother have need, and shutteth up his bowels of compassion from him, how dwelleth
the love of God in him? My little children, let
us not love in word, neither in tongue; but in
deed and in truth. 1 John 3:16-18

📖 ENDURE TRIALS AND TRIBULATIONS

But the salvation of the righteous is of the
LORD: he is their strength in the time of trouble. And the LORD shall help them, and deliver them: he shall deliver them from the
wicked, and save them, because they trust in
him. Psalm 37:39-40

My brethren, count it all joy when ye fall into
divers temptations. Knowing this, that the
trying of your faith worketh patience. But let
patience have her perfect work, that ye may
be perfect and entire, wanting nothing.
James 1:2-4

Many are the afflictions of the righteous: but the LORD delivereth him out of them all.

Psalm 34:19

Because he hath set his love upon me, therefore will I deliver him…He shall call upon me, and I will answer him: I will be with him in trouble; I will deliver him, and honor him.

Psalm 91:14-15

When thou passest through the waters, I will be with thee; and through the rivers, they shall not overflow thee: when thou walkest through the fire, thou shalt not be burned; neither shall the flame kindle upon thee. For I am the LORD thy God, the Holy One of Israel, thy Savior.

Isaiah 43:2-3

These things I have spoken unto you, that in me ye might have peace. In the world ye shall have tribulation: but be of good cheer; I have overcome the world.

John 16:33

And not only so, but we glory in tribulations also: knowing that tribulation worketh patience.

Romans 5:3

To an inheritance incorruptible, and undefiled, and that fadeth not away, reserved in heaven for you, Who are kept by the power of God through faith unto salvation ready to be revealed in the last time. Wherein ye greatly rejoice, though now for a season, if need be, ye are in heaviness through manifold temptations, That the trial of your faith, being much more precious than of gold that perisheth, though it be tried with fire, might be found unto praise and honor and glory at the appearing of Jesus Christ.   1 Peter 1:4-7

So that we ourselves glory in you in the churches of God for your patience and faith in all your persecutions and tribulations that ye endure: Which is a manifest token of the righteous judgment of God, that ye may be counted worthy of the kingdom of God, for which ye also suffer...When he shall come to be glorified in his saints, and to be admired in all them that believe (because our testimony among you was believed) in that day. Wherefore also we pray always for you, that our God would count you worthy of this calling, and fulfill all the good pleasure of his goodness, and the work of faith with power. That the name of our Lord Jesus Christ may be glorified in you, and ye in him, according to the grace of our God and the Lord Jesus Christ.   2 Thessalonians 1:4-5, 10-12

God is our refuge and strength, a very present help in trouble.   Psalm 46:1

📖 FEAR THE LORD

Oh how great is thy goodness, which thou hast laid up for them that fear thee; which thou hast wrought for them that trust in thee before the sons of men!   Psalm 31:19

The angel of the LORD encampeth round about them that fear him, and delivereth them....O fear the LORD, ye his saints: for there is no want to them that fear him.

Psalm 34:7, 9

Blessed is the man that feareth the LORD, that delighteth greatly in his commandments. His seed shall be mighty upon earth: the generation of the upright shall be blessed. Wealth and riches shall be in his house: and his righteousness endureth for ever.   Psalm 112:1-3

In the fear of the LORD is strong confidence: and his children shall have a place of refuge. The fear of the LORD is a fountain of life, to depart from the snares of death.

Proverbs 14:26-27

For Those Who...

What man is he that feareth the LORD? him shall he teach in the way that he shall choose. His soul shall dwell at ease; and his seed shall inherit the earth.   Psalm 25:12-13

Behold, the eye of the LORD is upon them that fear him, upon them that hope in his mercy.
                                        Psalm 33:18

Like as a father pitieth his children, so the LORD pitieth them that fear him.   Psalm 103:13

Ye that fear the LORD, trust in the LORD: he is their help and their shield. The LORD hath been mindful of us: he will bless us; he will bless the house of Israel; he will bless the house of Aaron. He will bless them that fear the LORD, both small and great. The LORD shall increase you more and more, you and your children.   Psalm 115:11-14

Blessed is every one that feareth the LORD; that walketh in his ways. For thou shalt eat the labor of thine hands: happy shalt thou be, and it shall be well with thee.   Psalm 128:1-2

The fear of the LORD prolongeth days: but the years of the wicked shall be shortened.
                                        Proverbs 10:27

And the LORD commanded us to do all these statutes, to fear the LORD our God, for our good always, that he might preserve us alive, as it is at this day.   Deuteronomy 6:24

For as the heaven is high above the earth, so great is his mercy toward them that fear him.
                                        Psalm 103:11

But in every nation he that feareth him, and worketh righteousness, is accepted with him.
                                        Acts 10:35

📖 GIVE TO OTHERS

Honor the LORD with thy substance, and with the firstfruits of all thine increase: So shall thy barns be filled with plenty, and thy presses shall burst out with new wine.   Proverbs 3:9-10

Every man according as he purposeth in his heart, so let him give; not grudgingly, or of necessity: for God loveth a cheerful giver.
                                        2 Corinthians 9:7

And God is able to make all grace abound toward you; that ye, always having all sufficiency in all things, may abound to every good work.   2 Corinthians 9:8

For Those Who...

The liberal soul shall be made fat: and he that watereth shall be watered also himself.

Proverbs 11:25

He that giveth unto the poor shall not lack.

Proverbs 28:27

Bring ye all the tithes into the storehouse, that there may be meat in mine house, and prove me now herewith, saith the LORD of hosts, if I will not open you the windows of heaven, and pour you out a blessing, that there shall not be room enough to receive it.

Malachi 3:10

Give, and it shall be given unto you; good measure, pressed down, and shaken together, and running over, shall men give into your bosom. For with the same measure that ye mete withal it shall be measured to you again.

Luke 6:38

Remember the words of the Lord Jesus, how he said, It is more blessed to give than to receive.

Acts 20:35

And he which soweth sparingly shall reap also sparingly; and he which soweth bountifully shall reap also bountifully.

2 Corinthians 9:6

📖 LOVE GOD

Know therefore that the LORD thy God, he is God, the faithful God, which keepeth covenant and mercy with them that love him and keep his commandments to a thousand generations. Deuteronomy 7:9

Because he hath set his love upon me, therefore will I deliver him: I will set him on high, because he hath known my name. He shall call upon me, and I will answer him: I will be with him in trouble; I will deliver him, and honor him. Psalm 91:14-15

If a man love me, he will keep my words: and my Father will love him, and we will come unto him, and make our abode with him. John 14:23

And we know that all things work together for good to them that love God, to them who are the called according to his purpose. Romans 8:28

Blessed is the man that endureth temptation: for when he is tried, he shall receive the crown of life, which the Lord hath promised to them that love him. James 1:12

For Those Who...

The LORD preserveth all them that love him: but all the wicked will he destroy.

Psalm 145:20

It is written, Eye hath not seen, nor ear heard, neither have entered into the heart of man, the things which God hath prepared for them that love him.

1 Corinthians 2:9

But if any man love God, the same is known of him.

1 Corinthians 8:3

📖 OBEY THE LORD

Blessed are they that hear the word of God, and keep it.

Luke 11:28

He that hath my commandments, and keepeth them, he it is that loveth me: and he that loveth me shall be loved of my Father, and I will love him, and will manifest myself to him.

John 14:21

And hereby we do know that we know him, if we keep his commandments...But whoso keepeth his word, in him verily is the love of God perfected: hereby know we that we are in him.

1 John 2:3, 5

Hear therefore, O Israel, and observe to do it; that it may be well with thee, and that ye may increase mightily, as the LORD God of thy fathers hath promised thee, in the land that floweth with milk and honey...And thou shalt do that which is right and good in the sight of the LORD: that it may be well with thee, and that thou mayest go in and possess the good land which the LORD sware unto thy fathers.   Deuteronomy 6:3, 18

See, I have set before thee this day life and good, and death and evil. In that I command thee this day to love the LORD thy God, to walk in his ways, and to keep his commandments and his statutes and his judgments, that thou mayest live and multiply: and the LORD thy God shall bless thee in the land whither thou goest to possess it.   Deuteronomy 30:15-16

Whosoever therefore shall break one of these least commandments, and shall teach men so, he shall be called the least in the kingdom of heaven: but whosoever shall do and teach them, the same shall be called great in the kingdom of heaven.   Matthew 5:19

Ye are my friends, if ye do whatsoever I command you.   John 15:14

For Those Who...

All the paths of the LORD are mercy and truth unto such as keep his covenant and his testimonies. Psalm 25:10

For whosoever shall do the will of my Father which is in heaven, the same is my brother, and sister, and mother. Matthew 12:50

And the world passeth away, and the lust thereof: but he that doeth the will of God abideth for ever. 1 John 2:17

📖 PRAY

If my people, which are called by my name, shall humble themselves, and pray, and seek my face, and turn from their wicked ways; then will I hear from heaven, and will forgive their sin, and will heal their land.
2 Chronicles 7:14

Be careful for nothing; but in every thing by prayer and supplication with thanksgiving let your requests be made known unto God. And the peace of God, which passeth all understanding, shall keep your hearts and minds through Christ Jesus.
Philippians 4:6-7

But thou, when thou prayest, enter into thy closet, and when thou hast shut thy door, pray to thy Father which is in secret; and thy Father which seeth in secret shall reward thee openly. Matthew 6:6

Ask, and it shall be given you; seek, and ye shall find; knock, and it shall be opened unto you: for every one that asketh receiveth; and he that seeketh findeth; and to him that knocketh it shall be opened. Matthew 7:7-8

If ye abide in me, and my words abide in you, ye shall ask what ye will, and it shall be done unto you. Herein is my Father glorified, that ye bear much fruit; so shall ye be my disciples. John 15:7-8

And the prayer of faith shall save the sick, and the Lord shall raise him up; and if he have committed sins, they shall be forgiven him. The effectual fervent prayer of a righteous man availeth much. James 5:15-16

But ye, beloved, building up yourselves on your most holy faith, praying in the Holy Ghost. Jude 20

For Those Who...

📖 Seek the Lord

But if from thence thou shalt seek the LORD thy God, thou shalt find him, if thou seek him with all thy heart and with all thy soul.

Deuteronomy 4:29

I sought the LORD, and he heard me, and delivered me from all my fears...The young lions do lack, and suffer hunger: but they that seek the LORD shall not want any good thing.

Psalm 34:4,10

Let all those that seek thee rejoice and be glad in thee: and let such as love thy salvation say continually, Let God be magnified. Psalm 70:4

I love them that love me; and those that seek me early shall find me. Proverbs 8:17

And ye shall seek me, and find me, when ye shall search for me with all your heart. And I will be found of you, saith the LORD.

Jeremiah 29:13-14

But without faith it is impossible to please him: for he that cometh to God must believe that he is, and that he is a rewarder of them that diligently seek him. Hebrews 11:6

The humble shall see this, and be glad: your heart shall live that seek God.   Psalm 69:32

But seek ye first the kingdom of God, and his righteousness; and all these things shall be added unto you.   Matthew 6:33

📖 SERVE GOD

If they obey and serve him, they shall spend their days in prosperity, and their years in pleasures.   Job 36:11

The LORD redeemeth the soul of his servants: and none of them that trust in him shall be desolate.   Psalm 34:22

Serve the LORD with gladness...For the LORD is good; his mercy is everlasting; and his truth endureth to all generations.   Psalm 100:2, 5

Present your bodies a living sacrifice, holy, acceptable unto God, which is your reasonable service. And be not conformed to this world: but be ye transformed by the renewing of your mind, that ye may prove what is that good, and acceptable, and perfect, will of God.   Romans 12:1-2

For Those Who...

If any man serve me, let him follow me; and where I am, there shall also my servant be: if any man serve me, him will my Father honor.

John 12:26

Therefore, my beloved brethren, be ye sted-fast, unmoveable, always abounding in the work of the Lord, forasmuch as ye know that your labor is not in vain in the Lord.

1 Corinthians 15:58

And whatsoever ye do, do it heartily, as to the Lord, and not unto men; Knowing that of the Lord ye shall receive the reward of the inheritance: for ye serve the Lord Christ.

Colossians 3:23-24

And there shall be no more curse: but the throne of God and of the Lamb shall be in it; and his servants shall serve him: And they shall see his face; and his name shall be in their foreheads.

Revelation 22:3-4

📖 SUFFER FOR CHRIST

And our hope of you is stedfast, knowing, that as ye are partakers of the sufferings, so shall ye be also of the consolation.

2 Corinthians 1:7

And he said to them all, If any man will come after me, let him deny himself, and take up his cross daily, and follow me. For whosoever will save his life shall lose it: but whosoever will lose his life for my sake, the same shall save it. Luke 9:23-24

If so be that we suffer with him, that we may be also glorified together. For I reckon that the sufferings of this present time are not worthy to be compared with the glory which shall be revealed in us. Romans 8:17-18

For our light affliction, which is but for a moment, worketh for us a far more exceeding and eternal weight of glory. 2 Corinthians 4:17

For what glory is it, if, when ye be buffeted for your faults, ye shall take it patiently? but if, when ye do well, and suffer for it, ye take it patiently, this is acceptable with God. 1 Peter 2:20

Which is a manifest token of the righteous judgment of God, that ye may be counted worthy of the kingdom of God, for which ye also suffer: Seeing it is a righteous thing with God to recompense tribulation to them that trouble you. 2 Thessalonians 1:5-6

For Those Who...

If ye be reproached for the name of Christ, happy are ye; for the spirit of glory and of God resteth upon you: on their part he is evil spoken of, but on your part he is glorified.

1 Peter 4:14

But the God of all grace, who hath called us unto his eternal glory by Christ Jesus, after that ye have suffered a while, make you perfect, stablish, strengthen, settle you.

1 Peter 5:10

📖 TRUST THE LORD

Our fathers trusted in thee: they trusted, and thou didst deliver them. They cried unto thee, and were delivered: they trusted in thee, and were not confounded.   Psalm 22:4-5

For our heart shall rejoice in him, because we have trusted in his holy name. Let thy mercy, O LORD, be upon us, according as we hope in thee.   Psalm 33:21-22

Trust in the LORD with all thine heart; and lean not unto thine own understanding. In all thy ways acknowledge him, and he shall direct thy paths.   Proverbs 3:5-6

And they that know thy name will put their trust in thee: for thou, LORD, hast not forsaken them that seek thee.   Psalm 9:10

Trust in the LORD, and do good; so shalt thou dwell in the land, and verily thou shalt be fed. Delight thyself also in the LORD; and he shall give thee the desires of thine heart. Commit thy way unto the LORD; trust also in him; and he shall bring it to pass. And he shall bring forth thy righteousness as the light, and thy judgment as the noonday.
                                             Psalm 37:3-6

Blessed is that man that maketh the LORD his trust, and respecteth not the proud, nor such as turn aside to lies.   Psalm 40:4

📖 WAIT ON GOD

The LORD is good unto them that wait for him, to the soul that seeketh him. It is good that a man should both hope and quietly wait for the salvation of the LORD.
                                      Lamentations 3:25-26

Wait on the LORD: be of good courage, and he shall strengthen thine heart: wait, I say, on the LORD.   Psalm 27:14

For Those Who...

Those that wait upon the LORD, they shall inherit the earth...Wait on the LORD, and keep his way, and he shall exalt thee to inherit the land: when the wicked are cut off, thou shalt see it. Psalm 37:9, 34

And therefore will the LORD wait, that he may be gracious unto you, and therefore will he be exalted, that he may have mercy upon you: for the LORD is a God of judgment: blessed are all they that wait for him. Isaiah 30:18

But they that wait upon the LORD shall renew their strength; they shall mount up with wings as eagles; they shall run, and not be weary; and they shall walk, and not faint.
Isaiah 40:31

For since the beginning of the world men have not heard, nor perceived by the ear, neither hath the eye seen, O God, beside thee, what he hath prepared for him that waiteth for him. Isaiah 64:4

WORK DILIGENTLY

Let not your hands be weak: for your work shall be rewarded. 2 Chronicles 15:7

Wealth gotten by vanity shall be diminished: but he that gathereth by labor shall increase.

Proverbs 13:11

In all labor there is profit.   Proverbs 14:23

The thoughts of the diligent tend only to plenteousness.   Proverbs 21:5

Seest thou a man diligent in his business? he shall stand before kings; he shall not stand before mean men.   Proverbs 22:29

Servants, be obedient to them that are your masters according to the flesh, with fear and trembling, in singleness of your heart, as unto Christ; Not with eyeservice, as menpleasers; but as the servants of Christ, doing the will of God from the heart; With good will doing service, as to the Lord, and not to men: Knowing that whatsoever good thing any man doeth, the same shall he receive of the Lord.   Ephesians 6:5-8

And whatsoever ye do, do it heartily, as to the Lord, and not unto men; Knowing that of the Lord ye shall receive the reward of the inheritance: for ye serve the Lord Christ.

Colossians 3:23-24

For Those Who...

A wise servant shall have rule over a son that causeth shame, and shall have part of the inheritance among the brethren.   Proverbs 17:2

Who then is a faithful and wise servant, whom his lord hath made ruler over his household, to give them meat in due season? Blessed is that servant, whom his lord when he cometh shall find so doing. Verily I say unto you, That he shall make him ruler over all his goods.   Matthew 24:45-47

His lord said unto him, Well done, thou good and faithful servant: thou hast been faithful over a few things, I will make thee ruler over many things: enter thou into the joy of thy lord.   Matthew 25:21

Let a man so account of us, as of the ministers of Christ, and stewards of the mysteries of God. Moreover it is required in stewards, that a man be found faithful...Then shall every man have praise of God.

1 Corinthians 4:1-2, 5

As every man hath received the gift, even so minister the same one to another, as good stewards of the manifold grace of God.

1 Peter 4:10

Study to show thyself approved unto God, a workman that needeth not to be ashamed, rightly dividing the word of truth.

2 Timothy 2:15

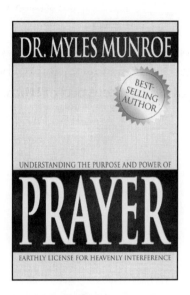

Understanding the Purpose and Power of Prayer
Dr. Myles Munroe

All that God is—and all that God has—may be received
through prayer. Everything you need to fulfill your purpose
on earth is available to you through prayer. The biblically
based, time-tested principles presented here by Dr. Myles
Munroe will ignite and transform the way you pray.
Be prepared to enter into a new dimension of faith,
a deeper revelation of God's love, and a renewed
understanding that you can pray—and receive results.

ISBN: 0-88368-442-X • Trade • 240 pages

W

WHITAKER
HOUSE

proclaiming the power of the Gospel through the written word
visit our website at www.whitakerhouse.com

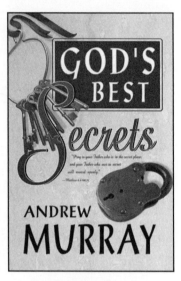

God's Best Secrets
Andrew Murray

From the Scriptures, Andrew Murray found out that every Christian can expect God to reveal Himself in an intimate, refreshing, powerful way. In this uplifting devotional, Murray shares the personal revelation that he gained from spending quiet time alone with God. Explore the secrets of fellowship, prayer, faith, and more as you enter into the wonderful privileges that are open to you. While you reflect on the inspirational thoughts presented here, you will discover many of *God's Best Secrets*.

ISBN: 0-88368-559-0 • Trade • 304 pages

lu

WHITAKER
HOUSE

proclaiming the power of the Gospel through the written word
visit our website at www.whitakerhouse.com

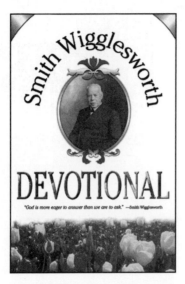

"God is more eager to answer than we are to ask." —Smith Wigglesworth

Smith Wigglesworth Devotional
Smith Wigglesworth

You are invited to journey with Smith Wigglesworth on a
year-long trip that will quench your spiritual thirst while it
radically transforms your faith. As you daily explore these
challenging insights from the Apostle of Faith, you will
connect with God's glorious power, cast out doubt, and
see impossibilities turn into realities. Your prayer life will
never be the same again when you personally experience
the joy of seeing awesome, powerful results
as you extend God's healing grace to others.

ISBN: 0-88368-574-4 • Trade • 560 pages

W
WHITAKER
HOUSE

proclaiming the power of the Gospel through the written word
visit our website at www.whitakerhouse.com

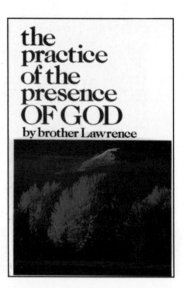

The Practice of the Presence of God
Brother Lawrence

Brother Lawrence was a man of humble beginnings who discovered the secret of living moment by moment with a sense of God's presence. It is the art of "practicing the presence of God in one single act that does not end." For nearly three hundred years, this unparalleled classic has given both blessing and instruction to millions who can be content with nothing less than knowing God in all His majesty and experiencing His loving presence throughout each day.

ISBN: 0-88368-105-6 • Pocket • 96 pages

WHITAKER
HOUSE

proclaiming the power of the Gospel through the written word
visit our website at www.whitakerhouse.com

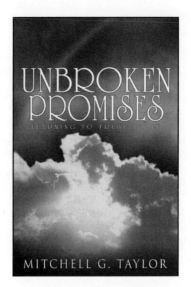

Unbroken Promises
Mitchell Taylor

We've all been disappointed by promises unkept. Our hearts have been broken by family, friends, coworkers, and even those in the church. We feel we can trust no one, and so we retreat into our fortresses of distrust and suspicion, guarding our hearts at all costs. Can we ever trust again? Yes, we can. But first we have to take down the self-made walls of protection surrounding our hearts. Discover the meaning of promises kept, the depths of God's faithfulness, and the true freedom that comes to those who surrender their fortresses of fear. You can learn to trust again!

ISBN: 0-88368-871-9 • Trade • 144 pages

W

WHITAKER
HOUSE

proclaiming the power of the Gospel through the written word
visit our website at www.whitakerhouse.com

You hunger to live in the presence of God. You yearn to know the Father's heart in an intimate way. You desire revelation and passionate encounters with the Almighty. You want to spend time away from the world, getting to know the Father in a deeper way. If you long to experience a greater intimacy with the Father, *The Secret Place* will draw you in and change your life!

The Secret Place: Passionately Pursuing His Presence
Dr. Dale A. Fife
ISBN: 0-88368-715-1 • Trade • 240 pages

The Hidden Kingdom: Journey into the Heart of God
Dr. Dale A. Fife
ISBN: 0-88368-947-2 • Trade • 256 pages

There are divine moments in life when you turn a corner and are astounded by unexpected, breathtaking vistas that you never imagined. Suddenly your world is changed forever. You have entered a supernatural realm, an eternal dimension, where Jesus is Lord and creation itself shouts His glory. The brilliantly illuminating revelation in *The Hidden Kingdom* will catapult you into such an experience. If you want an empowered life, this book will lead you on a journey into the heart of God.